LAKE MANYARA
NATIONAL PARK

Published in 2006 by:
Gallery Publications
P O Box 3181, Zanzibar, Tanzania
Email: gallery@swahilicoast.com

© Gallery Publications
Text by Graham Mercer
Edited by Vanessa Beddoe
Photographs by © Javed Jafferji unless indicated
Designed by Ali Khamis

ISBN: 9987 667 50 3

Acknowledgements

The author and photographer would like to thank the Tanzanian Minister for Natural Resources and Tourism, the Rt Hon Zakia Meghji MP, who has done so much to promote her country's outstanding national parks and reserves; all those people at the Tanzanian National Parks Authority who have helped in this project, including James Lembeli (Public Relations Manager), Mrs Kibasa, Chief Park Warden, Manyara, Mr Seth Mihayo and all rangers and office staff; Mr Richard Gomes of Serena Hotels, Arusha and all management and staff of the excellent Serena Hotel, Manyara; Shayne Richardson and Duncan Butchart of Conservation Corporation Africa (Conscorp); Debra Fox (Director) and Head Ranger Abdallah Hassan, of Conscorp's Tree Lodge, Manyara; the Lake Manyara Hotel; Kirurumu Tented Lodge and Migunga Camp, Manyara; the late Dr Desmond Vesey-Fitzgerald, eminent and generous-hearted naturalist who introduced me to Manyara; Iain (now Dr) Douglas-Hamilton, who obligingly tried to scare the living daylights out of me many years ago, with some success, when introducing me to some of his beloved elephants in Manyara; David Marsh, whose passion for northern Tanzania is evident in the excellent website he runs; all staff at the Twiga Guest House and Camping Site, Mto wa Mbu; Mr John Gadafi, Cultural Tour guide in Mto wa Mbu and friend Bakari; the Board, CEO and staff of the International School of Tanganyika, Dar es Salaam; Gloria Mawji and last but not least the author's wife Anjum and other safari partners who have shared so many memorable times in Manyara. One such companion, Barry Whittemore, kindly contributed the paragraphs on Manyara's birds, for which special thanks. Special thanks also to the photographer's wife Kulsum Jafferji, his sons Kumail and Hasnain Jafferji and parents Abid and Bashira Jafferji for supporting with ideas and projects.

This book is dedicated to the wildlife and people of Lake Manyara.

LAKE MANYARA
NATIONAL PARK

Graham Mercer • Javed Jafferji

Published by
Gallery Publications

CONTENTS

Left: Olive baboons feeding by the Msasa River
Next: Cow and calf elephants by a Manyara track
Next: Buffalo bath time, Lake Manyara
Next: Manyara's party piece - lions in trees
Next: Sharp-tasting snack at the Thorn Tree Café

INTRODUCTION

Manyara is something of a Cinderella among the northern national parks, with one big difference: her sisters are attractive, not ugly. Not that Manyara itself isn't attractive; its situation beneath the precipitous western wall of the Great Rift, and the presence of the beautiful lake from which it takes its name, ensure plenty of admirers. But far too many safari companies, in their eagerness to show their clients the "belles of the ball' further up the road, Ngorongoro and the Serengeti, tend to overlook the beauty closer to home.

This is unfortunate, for like many Cinderellas Manyara is more than just a pretty face, as a longer acquaintance would confirm. Its 330 sq km, relatively few by African standards, encompass seven distinct wildlife habitats (including 230 km of the lake), a greater topographical and biological diversity, within such a limited space, than is found in any other Tanzanian park. Which is one reason why Manyara is listed by the UN as a World Biosphere Reserve, the aims of which are to reconcile conservation of biodiversity with its

Left: Lake Manyara, beautiful Cinderella of the Northern Circuit

sustainable use, through conservation, development and logistical support. Cindrella has found a Fairy Godmother.

Though the park (excluding the lake) is at no point wider than 10 km, its vegetation can be dense in places, making game-viewing difficult. But this should be seen as a challenge, not a deterrent. In fact Manyara is in many ways far more typical of Tanzania's parks than the Serengeti Plains or Ngorongoro Crater floor, where you can see a four-striped grass mouse a mile away (or so it sometimes seems). You have to work harder in Manyara; it demands involvement. Given this, and the willingness and humility to learn, you will discover the pleasures and satisfactions that come with commitment, patience and well-applied bushcraft.

But it is better to pop into Manyara, at least as far as the Hippo Pool, than not pop in at all. Don't be tempted to drive past, for the Hippo Pool is only a short drive away, and as good a place as any from which to enjoy Manyara's more immediate attractions. The lake's shallows, beyond the Simba River (of which the Hippo Pools are a natural part) seethe with waterfowl and waders, especially in the northern winter, and in places flamingos, feeding in great crescentic concentrations, softened by haze and their own distorted reflections, can seem from a distance to be mirror-images of clouds, pinkened by the sun.

At least 35 species of birds can usually be seen on and around the Hippo Pool, more than most people would normally see in a whole year in a European garden. What you won't see in a European garden, which you will see here, are lots of hippos, often out of the water. And almost certainly there will be impalas at the edge of the nearby woodland, chestnut flanks gleaming, and giraffes, buffalos, zebras and wildebeeste out on the saline, short-grass margins of the lake. And maybe one or two of Manyara's many elephants. It is here that first-time visitors will experience that sometimes surprising truth about the bush, for contrary to the impression given by many wildlife films, the bush is overwhelmingly tranquil, a serenity that can soothe body and soul.

The tranquility is deceptive, the tranquility of opposing forces in balance. For the animals peacefully feeding or resting it is the poise of the tightrope walker. Except that the bush has no safety net; creatures which fall off the high wire don't climb back. This is the darker side of the bush, but no less natural. It doesn't show itself as often as many newcomers might imagine, but if it does, regard

yourself as fortunate to witness such dramatic events, safe inside your vehicle. For the animals themselves it is simply a matter of life and death.

But it is life which this little book celebrates; your own, for once inside the park you become part of it, and the life around you. Hopefully, this booklet will prove to be, in the words of the original booklets, "A guide to your increased enjoyment". 1960s words, these, from a more light-hearted era; too many of us now take life too seriously. There is much to be serious about in Manyara, but the most important thing, on any safari, is to enjoy it. If you don't enjoy Manyara, the Cinderella of the North, this book will have failed, and so, perhaps, will you; if you want to dance with Cinderella, you first have to get to know her...

Top: Wildebeest in the Hippo Pool area

HISTORY

The Manyara region was only settled during the 20th century, and made known to the outside world through the Vienna-born explorer and geographer Oscar Baumann, after his "Massai Expedition" of 1891/93, which involved 200 men, women and children, and took Baumann from the coast to Lakes Tanganyika and Victoria, and to what is now Rwanda and Burundi. During this time he mapped, at first hand, much of what is now Tanzania, and his interest in local peoples, together with his low-key, entertaining style of writing, did much to bring the areas he covered into focus throughout Europe and elsewhere.

Baumann and his great entourage filed through what is now the national park en route from the nearby Mbugwe homelands to Ngorongoro and the Serengeti. Interestingly, Baumann makes no mention of any wildlife in the area; rinderpest, a highly contagious and deadly disease which affects many wild ungulates (hoofed animals) as well as domestic stock, was certainly raging through nearby Ngorongoro,

---

Left: Lake Manyara as it might have looked during its formation

though even if Manyara had been badly affected one would have thought that Baumann would have seen enough game to pass comment.

Certainly the area was rich in game a few decades later, when it became a favourite destination among trophy hunters such as the writer Ernest Hemingway, whose ultra-macho lifestyle doesn't always endear him to New Age generations. But love him or loathe him, Hemingway was an outstanding and influential writer. In *The Green Hills of Africa* he describes Manyara (in 1935) as;

"...a green, pleasant country with hills below the forest that grew thick on the side of the mountain, and it was cut by the valleys of several watercourses that came down out of the thick timber on the mountain...If you looked away from the forest and the mountain side you could follow the watercourses and the hilly slope of the land down until the land flattened and the grass was brown and burned and, away, across a long sweep of country, was the brown Rift Valley and the shine of Lake Manyara."

In the same year it was suggest-

ed that this attractive, game-rich area be made into a national park, but this was rejected by the governor of the time, who described the western lakeshore as "one of the richest agricultural areas in the Territory". It is obvious from the following quotation, however, taken from the *Tanganyika Guide* in 1948, that Manyara was not only still full of game but that wildlife photography was becoming popular. The first two lines refer to the Engaruka area, the rest Manyara:

"During a stay of a week in this neighbourhood lion, zebra, Grant's and Thomson's gazelle, impala, wildebeest, rhinoceros, oryx and gerenuk may be obtained.

From here Maji Moto, sixty miles south along the Rift Wall, may be visited. The hot springs there seem to be a natural spa for wild life and there will be found spoor of elephant, rhinoceros, buffalo, lion and all kinds of smaller game. The place is a game photographer's paradise.

Lake Manyara, seen from the hot springs, has a great variety of birds, including thousands of flamingos."

In 1957 Manyara was proclaimed a Game Reserve and in 1960 a national park. Its name was

Left: Oscar Baumann with African attendants
Top: "Game photographer's paradise" - close to Maji Moto

taken from a Maasai word, *eman-yara,* for the plant *Eurphorbia tiru-calli,* common in the area and often used by the Maasai as a stock-proof hedge for their encampments. In the late 1960s its elephants were the subject of an important study by Iain Douglas-Hamilton, who together with his wife Oria did much to enhance the park's popularity through their book *Among the Elephants* and associated film documentaries. In 1971 Peter Matthiessen, in *The Tree Where Man Was Born,* described Manyara as "the best place to watch elephants in the world", a highly subjective opinion but in terms of elephant densities quite valid; a decade later a total of 613 elephants was estimated, something like six per square kilometre, twice the human population density of Australia or Canada.

By 1985, according to Boyd Norton in *The African Elephant: Last Days of Eden* the elephant population was down to around 450 and by 1991 as low as 150. Such figures are to be regarded with caution, as elephants, despite their size, are not easy to count in thick forest, and they often move in and out of a particular park. But heavy, organized poaching undoubtedly devastated elephant populations throughout East Africa during the late 1970s and the 1980s. And brought

the Black Rhino to extinction in many so-called sanctuaries, including Manyara.

The Lake Manyara Hotel was built on the top of the Rift wall, overlooking the lake, in the 1960s. Towards the end of the 20th century the luxury Lake Manyara Serena Safari Lodge and Kirirumu Tented Camp were also built on the edge of the escarpment, further north, and Migunga Tented Camp was established on the Rift floor, just outside the park, close to the village of Mto wa Mbu. In 2002 the Lake Manyara Tree Lodge, another "high-end" establishment, replaced the Maji Moto Camp at the extreme southern end of the park itself. Meanwhile a tourist-class lodge, E Unoto, has opened in Maasai country half-an-hour's drive to the north of the park gates, and Mto wa Mbu, originating in the early decades of the 20th century, has grown into a large and still-expanding village, providing low-cost but very reasonable accommodation in the form of guest houses and camping sites.

Left: Manyara - "the best place to watch elephants in the world"?
Top: The pool at Serena Safari Lodge

MANYARA'S GEOGRAPHY, VEGETATION AND CLIMATE

Location, location, location…

Manyara's location is as splendid as it is fascinating; few national parks can have had such a dramatic geological history or have undergone such an astounding transformation from the turbulence of its past to the tranquility of its present.

The causes of that turbulence, though it takes imagination to picture how it would have been at the time, are obvious long before you reach the park gate, assuming you drive or fly from Arusha. For Arusha itself (where most safaris to Manyara begin) lies at the foot of an extinct volcano, and whether you travel by road or by air, the country through or over which you pass is defined and shaped by its volcanic counterparts.

By road the main park gate is 117 km from Arusha, by air 93 km due west. The first 81 km of the road take you across the Ardai plains to Makayuni, a small settlement at the north-western corner of the so-called Maasai Steppe, at the eastern edge of the Rift Valley. Until recently

Left: Drowned trees close to the Hippo Pool

Makayuni also stood at the eastern end of a rocky, corrugated and often dusty road which was capable of inspiring dread, even among old Africa hands, and which must surely have resulted, among women passengers in the latter stages of pregnancy, in several premature births.

Old Africa hands, pregnant ladies and passengers in general can now rest assured, literally as well as metaphorically. This final 36 km of their journey to Manyara has been tamed by tarmac, and is currently (2005) one of the best roads in Tanzania, making Manyara more easily accessible by vehicle than ever, and giving travellers time, and peace-of-mind, to appreciate the significance of what they are doing, for in driving from Makayuni to Manyara they are crossing one of the Earth's most interesting, and in parts most beautiful, natural features, the Great Rift Valley.

Geography

One would think that by now the dimensions and age of such a prominent scar on the surface of the Earth would be relatively well established, but depending on which Internet websites one believes, the length of the Valley alone varies from less than 5,000 km to almost 10,000, suggesting that the feature is rather more elastic than rift valleys ought to be. It has a highly mobile birthday also, but this guide (and its author) are hardly qualified to comment upon that.

Suffice to say that the word "Great", as usually applied to the Rift, is not inappropriate; the valley stretches from Syria to Mozambique, branching within East Africa to form eastern and western arms. And that it was probably formed 10 – 20 million years ago, due to the sliding apart of tectonic plates and the resulting subsidence. Basically the bottom fell out of a section of the Earth's crust. Lava flowed out and in some cases formed volcanoes; the Rift was littered with these orphans of violence, one of which, *Ol Doinyo Lengai* ("Mountain of God" to the Maasai) is still active, just 73 km from the entrance to Manyara. Now and again visitors to the park will be reminded that they are in an earthquake zone. You needn't worry about such tremors, though if you happen to coincide with one the phrase "Did the Earth move for you?" might take on more literal connotations.

"Littered" might be a suitable way of describing the initial and seemingly arbitrary upheavals, but it hardly applies now, for the "orphans of violence" have matured, moulded by the elements

into one of the most starkly beautiful parts of the planet. The Rift Valley around Manyara, with the lake and the western wall and the nearby heights of *Esimingor* as its focal points, and further north, around Lengai and Kerimasi, Kitumbeni and Gelai, is graced, rather than littered, with the manifestations of past violence.

Long before the traveller from Makayuni reaches Mto wa Mbu he or she will see "...the shine of Lake Manyara" as Hemingway called it, backed by the western wall, for the east-west crossing of the Rift is a gentle descent, the earth's crust having fallen at an angle towards the west here, rather than horizontally between two walls, as is the case further north.

But with every kilometre the escarpment dominates the western horizon, eventually obscuring the Crater highlands beyond, as the scarp rises, in this region, to an average of 427 m (1,400 feet) above the valley floor, itself (at the lake) 945 m above sea level. This wall of rock acts as a natural division between highlands and lowlands, and between high and low rainfalls respectively.

As the Rift was created streams cascaded down the western wall (as they still do, though many are seasonal) and as there was no outflow, a lake quickly formed. It is said to have reached its largest size

---

Top: Ol Donyo Lengai, the "Mountain of God"

250,000 years ago, stretching east-wards as far as Makayuni. These days it is normally about 15 km wide, 50 km long and surprisingly shallow, with a maximum depth of about three metres. Water from the surrounding plains, as well as from the Rift wall, seeps into it.

The lake comprises 70% of the park as it stands today (June 2005), though statistics vary from season to season as the lake expands and contracts. In 1961, for example, it was possible to drive across the lake bed, and in 1994 it was again reduced to a highly toxic puddle, thanks to drought and a high concentration of volcanic minerals. Yet in 1996 there was so much rainfall that the lake rose rapidly, washing away most of Maji Moto Camp, beyond the Hot Springs, and flooding much of the main track. At such times many trees are often killed by the unusually high water table, evidence of which can presently be seen close to the Hippo Pool on the Simba River. Typically the size of the lake varies between less drastic extremes.

Manyara, like most Rift Valley lakes, is alkaline, rich in phosphates and sulphates, though not as hostile an environment as certain other Rift lakes. In fact its mineral salts, concentrated by evaporation, provide a perfect if unlikely-seeming home for the algae which thrive in such conditions, and which in turn attract great flocks of flamingos.

The rest of the present park consists of most of the Rift wall itself, and the strip of land between the wall and the lake, a very small area when compared with other Tanzanian parks. But that narrow strip, some 50 km long, is home to one of the heaviest densities of wildlife in the world, and a great diversity of plants, habitats and scenery.

The face of the escarpment is steep and rugged in places. In other areas, where the gradient is more gentle, there are networks of animal tracks, evidence of the great biomass of animals mentioned above. The wall is cleft here and there by gorges, down which various watercourses, when in flow, cascade, before fetching up in the lake. The rock at the northern end of the park is volcanic and porous, allowing water to seep down through the Rift wall and emerge, where it meets an underlying, non-porous layer of ancient crystalline rock, as springs and streams at the base of the scarp.

Further south, around the Msasa River, this hard and unyielding crystalline rock is found at or just below the surface, permitting fewer springs and streams, except for those such as the Ndala, Bagayo and Endabash, which flow above ground down the entire face of the scarp. Further south still there are hot springs.

Left: The rugged escarpment rises from the fringes of the lake

Vegetation

These different geological conditions give rise to different types of vegetation. The porous rock at the northern end, with its resulting springs and streams, allows a high water table to be maintained, supporting a wonderfully mature, evergreen "groundwater" forest, the name arising from the nature of its sustenance. It is one of the few remaining groundwater forests in the Rift Valley, and unusual in that groundwater forests are normally found only in highland areas or in areas of much higher rainfall.

The trees found in the forest (brace yourself for their classical names in the interest of accuracy!) are dominated in numerical terms by *Croton macrostachys,* but among the trees which are perhaps more eye-catching are Cape mahogany *(Trichelia emetica),* the false mvule *(Antiaris toxicaria), Bridelia micrantha,* the so-called "quinine tree" *(Rauvolfia caffra),* a wild mango, *Tabernaemontana usambarensis),* sycamore fig *(Ficus sycamorus),* tamarind *(Tamarindus indica)* and sausage trees *(Kigelia africana).* Some of these trees are found here and there outside the forest also, especially along the various watercourses. Within the forest, where the water table is too high for forest trees to flourish, there are occasional swampy glades,

dominated by the tall reeds *Typha angustifolia* and *Cyperus immensus* and edged with star-grass *(Cynodon dactylon).* One dense swamp has reappeared at the north-western corner of the lake after many years, illustrating the changing nature of all wild places.

The groundwater forest is fringed along its southern edges by stands of yellow-barked acacias *(Acacia xanthophloea)* and wild date palm *(Phoenix reclinata).* Beyond these irregular boundaries the for-

est phases into a large extent of acacia woodland, in which the "Umbrella Thorn" *(Acacia tortilis)*, so often associated with East Africa, is most conspicuous. Another spiny tree, the "Desert Date" *(Balanites aegyptiaca)* is found in this woodland, along with various shrubs including *Cordia africana, Salvadora persica* and a wild gardenia *(Gardenia jovis-tonantis)*.

The acacias eventually give way to more nondescript, open country of low bush, scrub and grassland, in the broad expanse of land bisected by the Endabash River. This country is characterized by a shrubby species of caper known as the "Woolly Caper Bush" *(Capparis tomentosa),* with patches of Paperbark Acacia (A. *siebriana)*. By the Hot Springs, the band of country between lake and scarp is squeezed into a narrow rocky passage at the foot of the

Top: Giraffes feeding below the escarpment (and Lake Manyara Hotel)

Rift wall, through which the track winds before penetrating another extent of *Acacia tortilis* and crossing the Yambi River to the lovely mahogany *(Trichelia emetica)* woodland beyond, in which Lake Manyara Tree Lodge is situated, and which marks the southern extreme of the park.

To one side of Manyara's ribbon of forest, woodland and bush lie the western flood-plains of the lake, curving with its contours between the soda flats and the bush, extending here and there in broad swathes, in other places quite narrow. These alkaline flood-plains, shorn by many herbivores, are populated by spike-seed grass *(Sporobolus spicatus)* and the sedge *Cyperus laevigatus,* both adapted to saline soils. The spike-seed is as tough and unfriendly as it sounds and the sedge tussocky, but Manyara's numerous buffalos, which feed extensively on the latter, trample both into ground-carpeting compliance.

The western boundary of Manyara's vegetational zone is composed of the plants growing on the Rift wall, significant among which is a hardy shrub, *Grewia tembensis,* a euphorbia *(E scheffleri),* a perennial herb, *Ruellia megachlamys,* and several aloes which thrive amid the steeper, rockier gradients. Another shrub, *Cadaba farinosa,* the starchy fruit of which is used, in southern Africa, as a standby in times of famine, is also found on the escarpment wall, as are the small trees *Terminalia brownii* and a species of *Commiphora*, and the massive baobab *(Adansonia digitata).*

Above the escarpment in the south, at the edge of the Mbulu

© Graham Mercer

Plateau, lies the Marang Forest, presently a protected reserve outside the park, though there are plans to include it. Its vegetation, which has been little studied, is the remnant of a once extensive highland forest, biologically similar to that on the eastern slopes of Ngorongoro Crater.

Climate

Manyara has a generally pleasant climate. Daytime temperatures can be high (occasionally reaching a maximum of 40° C during January and February) but the mean annual temperature is 22° C, with a minimum of 15° during the cooler months (mid-May to mid-November, with July the coolest).

At these cooler times of year sweaters, safari vests or even jackets are often needed in the mornings and evenings.

Manyara's proximity to the equator ensures two rainy seasons, the short (November/December) and the long (mid-March to mid-May), though rains vary from year to year in timings and intensity. The main dry season (June to October inclusive) coincides with the cooler months, though much of the hottest months (January/February) is also typically dry.

Left: Fascinating vegetation at the top of the Rift wall
Top: Don't worry - the rains are not usually so drastic!

PEOPLE AND CULTURE

The Arusha and Maasai

The Arusha and Maasai peoples are closely related, speaking the same language and sharing many traditions, and to most outsiders indistinguishable. In fact the Arusha are best regarded as one of several Maasai clans. It is probably still true, however, that they have taken to cultivation far more readily and completely (despite the fact that many Arusha keep cattle) while traditional Maasai remain purely pastoralist.

People driving from Arusha to Manyara will see many signs of cultivation and mixed farming along the way, especially in the early part of the journey. Many farms and settlements belong to the Arusha, though Maasai are plentiful around Monduli, a Maasai administrative centre. Until recently it was possible for outsiders to distinguish between the two groups by means of their traditional homes, which in the case of the Arusha were circular with thatched roofs, while the Maasai built low, loaf-shaped huts, entirely of saplings and mud, plastered with cow dung. The

Left: Newly-circumcised Maasai youth in post-circumcision black (the white facial markings symbolise milk)

houses of both groups were, and traditionally still are, arranged in a circle, usually enclosed within a circular thorn or euphorbia "*boma*" or hedge. These days, however, more and more Maasai, where the two peoples live close to each other, are adopting the round huts of their cousins.

The more traditional Maasai are to be found mainly in and around the Rift Valley, on the "Maasai Steppe" to the south of the main Moshi-Arusha-Makayuni road and throughout the Ngorongoro Conservation Area. They are probably the best-known, most photographed, most written-about people in East Africa, but in Tanzania very much in a minority in terms of numbers, one of 120 other tribes, the over-whelming majority of which are of Bantu cultivator origins.

The Maasai are undeniably colourful, though their reputation as a warrior race has been exaggerated, and tends to date back to the latter part of the nineteenth century, when Maasai clans, hungry for pasture, sometimes fought each other. They did, of course, wage war on neighbouring tribes for much the same reason, and were certainly much feared across a huge swathe of East Africa, but most of the fighting was in the form of cattle-raids and skirmishes, not battles for military supremacy. And although it is true that young Maasai *morani* (Swahili for men of the warrior age-grade) would sometimes sally forth to kill lions with spears to prove themselves, this is not practised nowadays, at least officially. Similarly, the much-remarked-upon habit of taking blood from a living cow, and drinking it (often with milk) is by no means an everyday occurrence.

Another common misunder-standing is that the Maasai are nomadic. During the course of their history they have wandered far south from their original homelands in what is now southern Sudan and part of the Nile basin (hence the term Nilotic), but once established in a certain area their movements became fairly predictable and seasonal, between dry and wet season pastures. In the old days they sometimes roamed widely, often to raid other tribes or clans, to grab cattle or retrieve their own, sometimes just for the hell of it.

None of this makes the Maasai less fascinating or (at times) formidable; to encounter a posse of Maasai *morani* in some of their wilder territory (such as out by Engaruka, north of Manyara) when they are in excitable mood can still bring uneasiness to the mind of the casual "intruder". But apart from confronting you in

their bold manner, and asking to be photographed (for a fee) they will, having satisfied their curiosity, stride off in their typically carefree, superior way, perhaps tossing their long-bladed spears ahead of them in sheer exuberance. And to remind you that you are among a very special people, who once struck terror into certain hearts.

The *morani* are part of a well-ordered, surprisingly democratic social system. Maasai life is a strict, male-orientated progression through various stages, each marked by important rituals, from the piercing of ear lobes and the knocking out of the two lower incisor teeth in childhood (to facil-itate feeding in the event of lock-jaw) through circumcision (girls as well as boys) after puberty, to adulthood, marriage and old age.

For the males there are four main stages, the "warrior" and "elder" grades each having junior and senior divisions. Young boys are expected to take care of the extended family's cattle, while girls help their mothers with household tasks and with milking. Traditionally the Maasai do not have chiefs. The elders have collective responsibility within a family group, wider issues being debated by neighbourhood committees of

Top: Maasai ceremonial artefacts

elders, often with guidance from the local *laibon,* a kind of senior advisor appointed for his wisdom and vision, and much respected.

As in most Tanzanian tribes women lead a hard life, especially after marriage, and life in a Maasai *enkang* is often far from idyllic. But Maasai women, with their heads shaven if married, and their typically colourful bead necklaces and ornaments, are amazingly long-suffering and good-natured, often with smiles (thanks to the staple Maasai diet of milk, milk and more milk!) that would depress a dentist. Or seduce a saint.

But to get to the heart of Maasai life you must understand their almost Hindu-like reverence for cattle (though the Maasai kill their cattle at times and relish the taste of beef). They believe, traditionally, that all the cattle on Earth were given to them by God (Enkai), and almost everything they do or say involves cattle, directly or otherwise. A Maasai elder in his *enkang* (or family enclosure) will proudly show off his herd to visitors, often knowing each animal by name and nature.

But Maasai society is changing, more quickly than ever. More and more Maasai farm their cattle commercially, selling surplus animals at local auctions. Many Maasai also now work in the cities, as accountants, computer technicians, administrators or whatever, dressed in smart western-style clothes. Others, especially the young "warriors", are giving up the old way of life to work as *askaris* (watchmen) in Dar es Salaam and Arusha and elsewhere, dressed in their traditional outfits and beads, their hair painstakingly fashioned into long braids, pinned into pigtails behind. Feared by would-be thieves and admired by tourists and expatriates (hence their popularity as watchmen) the young men often return to their native grasslands when they have saved enough money to set themselves up with cattle and/or a wife.

The best way for short-term visitors to learn something about traditional Maasai life is to visit one of their "cultural villages", an authentic working *"enkang"* which in return for certain fees welcomes outsiders. Such villages (including some Arusha) exist along the road between Arusha and Manyara, especially in the Rift itself, and many safari companies include cultural tours as part of their package. These visits only give a brief insight into the complex Maasai culture, but the observant visitor will learn a lot, and hopefully come away inspired to read more about these captivating people.

The Iraqw

You might hear (even from some Iraqw) that this other non-Bantu tribe actually originated in Iraq. In reality the two names are unconnected, though some authorities believe that the Iraqw

did originate in Arabia, in the Yemen. What is more certain is that at some point they spread south from the area we now know as Ethiopia. They are a Cushitic people, "Cushitic" being essentially a linguistic distinction, referring to a language group which developed in ancient times in the Horn of Africa.

The date of their arrival in what is now northern Tanzania isn't clear; estimates seem to vary between 200 and 2000 years ago, which doesn't exactly fill one with confidence in their accuracy. It is interesting, however, that Henry Fosbrooke, first Conservator of Ngorongoro and distinguished anthropologist, in his book *Ngorongoro: the Eighth Wonder,* makes no mention of such a date. What he does mention is that in 1934 "there was not a sign of habitation from Mto wa Mbu to Karatu, whilst the big triangle of superb land lying between the Rift and the forest edge, called Mbulumbulu, was entirely empty". This whole area is now heavily populated by Iraqw, whose average household (in 1999) numbered 7.6 members, with half the population under 15.

The Iraq are said to have entered the highlands, from the south, at some time during the

19th century to escape harassment by the Maasai. In the early 20th century, presumably reassured by the safety offered by German rule, they began to spread slowly across the highland plateau. In the mid-1920s a number of German settlers, their farms confiscated by the British during the First World War, were allowed to return, and began to carve out new coffee farms around Oldeani Mountain. This encouraged many Iraqw to move further north, first as labourers on the settlers' estates, eventually as farmers in their own right. This process accelerated during and after the Second World War, with German farms again being confiscated, at a time when food production was vital. The Iraqw helped to fill the vacuum.

Being experienced mixed farmers rather than pastoralists they made good use of the rich volcanic soils, and still do. Traditionally their settlements are organized in neighbourhood groups, the largest territorial unit, known as the *aya*, embracing several hamlets, or *hhay*. The farmers trade maize and tobacco with the neighbouring, pastoralist Datoga, from whom they buy cattle and various iron implements. They also exchange tobacco for honey, obtained from the wild by the hunter-gathering Hadzabe, who live by Lake Eyasi, and trade with various Bantu peoples on and around the plateau.

Iraqw society, like that of the Maasai and Datoga, is based on an age-grade system, male elders making decisions locally and committees of elders at community level. As with the Maasai there is a "father figure" (known by the Iraqw as the *qualarmo*) to whom these committees, via a religious leader-cum-spokesman, can turn for advice. The religious leader *(kahamusmo)* is widely respected, like the Maasai *laibon*, but his powers are restricted by the council of elders. Again like the Maasai, women in Iraqw society have a hard life of domestic toil, though role-sharing between husbands and wives is slowly becoming more acceptable, and women, who have their own informal organisations, often attend public village meetings.

Many tourists, and other visitors to Manyara, will encounter the Iraqw in the form of staff members of the various lodges, hotels, camps etc, but once again one of the best ways to get to know a little about them is to visit one of their "cultural villages" on the plateau, or take a similar tour from Mto wa Mbu.

Left: It is not known when the Iraqw arrived in northern Tanzania

Ethnic Mix – Mto wa Mbu

Mto wa Mbu, (Mosquito River), was for many years regarded by old Africa hands as a blot on the otherwise splendid landscape, but the village serves a very useful purpose, catering to tourists, especially at the low budget end of the market, with its various guest houses, camp sites, cafes, bars, filling stations, *dukas* (small shops), fruit, meat and curio markets and "mango tree *fundis*" (back-street car mechanics).

It is one of the best places in Tanzania in which to see or meet some of the country's 120 ethic groups. You won't find representatives of all 120, but you will find a good many, including Maasai, Arusha, Iraqw, Irangi, Chagga, Gogo, Mbugwe, Sonjo and others. There is a cultural tour office by the main road, where you can hire

decline to be photographed don't insist. In practice you should find that most people don't mind. The tour is worth taking for this reason alone, for taking photographs independently can be frustratingly time-consuming and often abortive or expensive.

Among the places you might visit are the local school, little back-street "breweries" where beer is made from bananas, and their adjacent and popular drinking parlours, various homesteads, *shambas* (small-holdings) and farms and of course the markets and dukas. But it is fascinating and enlightening just to walk along the road or down the side-streets with someone who knows the village.

If you have your own vehicle the guides will sometimes agree (for a fee) to accompany you to nearby Maasai or Arusha *enkang,* or take you up the escarpment into the Mbulumbulu Triangle, where you will be shown around various Iraqw settlements and often welcomed inside their thatched huts. The precautions mentioned above should be observed. As with all guided tours tips for the guide, if merited, are always welcome at the end.

guides to show you around the village. Such a tour is recommended, but make sure the guide is official, as part of the proceeds is meant to go into the village fund. Also make sure that you and he can communicate, and that you know, before setting off, what you are paying for and exactly how much. The fee should include the right to take photographs without extra charge, though if certain individuals

Left: Cultural tours to traditional villages are easily arranged

SPECIAL FEATURE MANYARA'S TREE CLIMBING LIONS

Manyara has long been known for its tree-climbing lions, and rightly so, for its lions readily climb trees. But the trees are more predictable (and more numerous) than the lions, which don't perform on cue like circus animals and which can seem, to visitors with high expectations and little time, terribly inconsiderate. So a little lowering of expectations (not hopes!) might be worthwhile.

Firstly, Manyara's lions are not unique. Lions in East Africa climb trees wherever lions and easily climbable trees are found. Secondly, there are only about 30-35 lions in Manyara at any one time, but there is, relative to the park's size, an awful lot of forest, woodland and bush. So the chances of finding lions in trees during a "quick flip" to the Hippo Pool and back are pretty low; some driver guides with years of experience have never seen lions in trees in Manyara. But it is also true that many safari companies (or their clients) often opt for the "quick flip" in Manyara, in their eagerness to spend more time in Ngorongoro and the Serengeti.

Left: Branch meeting of the local pride

You might be one of the lucky visitors who see lions in trees on their one-and-only visit, a short drive from the gate or the popular Hippo Pool. But the best ways to increase your chances are obvious; go to Manyara more often, stay there longer and spend more time looking, in appropriate areas, more carefully. Not everyone can afford to do this, of course, but if you can, the law of averages will eventually work to your advantage. And even if you don't see lions in trees, you will see much else that you would otherwise have missed. So try not to be too disappointed if you're unlucky; it's as good a reason as any for returning to Manyara one day, to spend more time there. Meanwhile, why do lions climb trees in the first place?

It makes more sense, perhaps, to ask why lions *wouldn't* climb trees. They are cats, after all, and although heavily built are quite capable of climbing trees (assuming the trees are easily climbable), and do so far more often than was once thought. But being cats they rarely expend energy unnecessarily; why climb a tree when you can flop down underneath one? Almost certainly there are several reasons. Lions don't like being pestered by biting flies, any more than we do, and like us they don't like getting wet or uncomfortably hot, which might explain why lions in many places seem to climb trees more often in the rainy season, when temperatures as well as rainfall are high and when tsetse flies are often more numerous. Amid

the branches they probably find some respite from the flies and the wet grass, and more of a breeze.

Apart from the wet grass, these reasons still hold good for the dry season, when flies don't disappear altogether and midday temperatures can still be uncomfortable at ground level. Certain trees also provide good look-out posts, especially when the grass down below is high. And in Manyara there is a more compelling reason for taking to the trees; the dense forest and woodland bustles with elephants and buffalos, so lying around on the ground, even for lions, is a little bit like humans trying to chill out on a beach while hordes of massive youths play football around them. There is another possibility; maybe lions actually enjoy climbing trees?

Two things are certain in Manyara. The lions do seem to spend more time in trees than lions elsewhere, sometimes among surprisingly dense and gloomy thickets. And their favoured perches in Manyara are up in the branches of the *Acacia tortilis* woodland which covers much of the park's central area, where many of the trees seem to have been designed with lions in mind. Manyara's lions do climb other trees, but it is among the lovely "umbrella thorns" that you are most likely to find them. Keep your eyes open, and look up as well as down.

Left: Lion cubs and their parents at play
Top: Chilling out (and out of harm's way) in an *Acacia tortilis*

THE PARK, ITS MAIN AREAS AND FLORA AND FAUNA

The groundwater forest

Visitors to Manyara enter via its northern gate (there is a gate in the south at Yambi but it is reserved for park officials) just beyond Mto wa Mbu. They find themselves suddenly immersed in the green gloom of the groundwater forest, as if they had fallen asleep in Mto wa Mbu and awoken in the Congo, but once their eyes have adjusted to the light the beauty and serenity of the forest are revealed. More observant visitors might notice a telling difference between the groundwater forest and true rainforest, as here in Manyara the trees are not festooned or clad with lichens and mosses, which absorb moisture from the air. The air here is relatively dry and rainfall relatively light (about 76.2 cm a year).

But the trees are no less fascinating, and among the most splendid is the Cape Mahogany, *Trichilea emetica*. A medium to tall evergreen (8–20 m) its timber, as one would expect from its common name, is used to make furniture, though of

Left: The luxuriant splendour of the groundwater forest

course the trees in Manyara are fully protected. The seeds of the mahogany produce high quality oil, used in soap-making, and the Pare people (who inhabit Tanzania's Pare Mountains) boil parts of its roots to treat stomach ache. Should you suffer from insomnia in Manyara, which is unlikely in the comfortable rooms of the lodges and camps, you might consider going to bed with a few *Trichilia* leaves, which are believed to induce sleep, though it might puzzle your room attendant the following morning...

Another fine tree found in the groundwater forest is the Sycamore Fig, *Ficus sycamorus,* the "sycamore" of the Bible. It varies from 5–25 m in height but mature trees can be identified by their distinctive yellow or yellow-green bark, and spreading branches bearing large, almost circular leaves, dark green and harsh to the touch. The fruits themselves are quite large for wild figs, up to 3 cm in diameter, in heavy, branched masses on the trunk and main branches, and yellowish to reddish when ripe. They are edible, and although often infested with insects are popular sources of food for various animals and birds, as are the highly nutritious leaves.

Several sycamore figs grow alongside the forest track, and among their sprawl of roots, or up

amid the branches feeding on the fruits, you will sometimes encounter a troop of Olive Baboons. Manyara has a particularly high number for its size and it is almost impossible to miss them here in the forest, where a large troop spends much of its time, its members often sitting on the track, grooming each other and periodically studying the passing tourists with their deep-set, rather "shrewd-looking" eyes. The Olive Baboon *(Papio anubis),* like other monkeys, is a highly social animal,

occurring in groups of 50 or more individuals, consisting of perhaps 7 or 8 males and approximately twice as many females, the balance being made up of juveniles at various stages of development.

Baboons usually leave their roosting sites, among the branches or cliffs, soon after sunrise, when they sit around grooming in small groups while the young ones play, before setting off to feed in appropriate trees or forage on the ground, in which case they travel in cohesive columns, fanning out to feed when circumstances are favourable. They are highly selective feeders, eating certain grasses, fruits, berries seeds (and their pods), leaves, roots, tubers and even bark. They are also known to eat insects, birds' eggs and young birds, and to kill and eat small mammals such as hares, vervet monkeys and young antelopes.

Male olive baboons, at up to 45 kg, are a third to half as big as

Top: Olive baboons are highly selective (and gregarious) feeders

females, their size exaggerated by their thick fur, especially around the mantle. And they can be very aggressive, among themselves and towards menacing predators; even leopards will often think twice about taking them on, not only because of the power of the big males, with their huge canines, but because of the collective power of the whole group, and the unholy fuss it creates when threatened.

But apart from a few outbreaks of squalling and squabbling, often among the youngsters, visitors to Manyara will normally see the baboons interacting peacefully, feeding, grooming or mating. Babies, like babies everywhere, are especially popular with human observers. For the first month or so of their lives they cling to Mum, quite literally when on the move, upside down under her stomach. At around 5 or 6 weeks the babies learn to cling to their mother's back with all four limbs, progressing, a few months later, to an upright position, riding jockey-fashion. Between 4 and 6 months

to be one of the invertebrates, young birds or even bushbabies on which they sometimes feed (like baboons they are mainly vegetarian, their diet including fruits, flowers and leaves). Again like baboons, they have cheek pouches, enabling them to "store" food as they forage and eat it later, at leisure. As they often eat some distance from their food source they indirectly do the forest a favour by distributing many of its seeds.

Blue monkeys, which often associate with other monkeys, are in Manyara generally seen in small groups of about 4-12, made up of females and young but often with only one adult male. Being diurnal their day begins as the morning light penetrates the forest, when males often make their explosive "pyoo" calls, rallying group members and warning other males to keep their distance. These calls are just one of a variety of vocalizations, some of which can fool inexperienced birders into thinking they have discovered an exciting new avian species! Feeding often begins high in the treetops, the monkeys descending into the lower, shadier tiers in the heat of the day before returning to the upper canopy later.

The Guernon monkeys, as the

they begin to spend most of their time with other juveniles.

Another primate often seen in the groundwater forest is the Blue Monkey *(Cercopithecus mitis)*, a lover of shade and well-watered habitats and therefore in its element here. Despite their common name the monkeys are predominantly dark grey, almost black, though in good light you will see that they have a bluish-grey mantle. Their Latin name, mitis, means "gentle" and the Blue Monkey certainly seems gentle enough, unless you happen

Cercopithecines are sometimes known ("guernon" meaning "fright" in French, due to the teeth-baring grimace that the monkeys sometimes exhibit) are all forest species except one. The forest guernons, including the Blue Monkey, are unique in that they progress through the trees by hurling themselves at convenient bunches of foliage rather than leaping from branch to branch, a somewhat precarious way to travel, one might think, though it seems to work. They come to the ground from time to time, when they feel secure, but are mainly arboreal.

You probably won't see too many birds as you pass through the forest, as they are relatively scarce, perhaps because the habitat is unsuitable for all but a few species, and/or because it harbours a high population of monkeys, which relish birds' eggs or fledglings. But one bird which is found there, the Silvery-cheeked Hornbill *(Bycanistes brevis),* is difficult to miss when it's around, partly because it is about 75 cm (2.5 feet) long with a wing-span of up to 1.8 metres (6 feet) and partly because it has a habit, even when hidden among the upper foliage of tall trees, of shattering the forest stillness with nasal brays and

Top: Silvery-cheeked Hornbill feeding on winged termites

grunts. Forest birds are often described as "shy and retiring" but this one isn't. Even when flying overhead it announces its presence by the rhythmic whoosh of its mighty wings.

The hornbills, which can seem almost completely black when seen in profile, have extensive areas of white on the back and rump, with white underwing coverts and white outer tail feathers, their black facial feathers being tipped with silvery-grey. But the most unusual feature of these (and many other) hornbills is the large casque (in this case dull cream in colour) which gives the group its collective name. The casque, mounted along the top of the upper mandible, is composed of keratin, and has little or no bone structure. More mysteriously, no one seems to know what its purpose is. Some biologists believe that it helps to strengthen the bill, which apparently is subjected to a lot of stress as hornbills have powerful jaws, though one might have thought that evolution could have simply designed a stronger bill. The cavity within the casque seems to indicate that it might be a sound chamber, but this has never been proved.

The hornbills spend most daylight hours in the forest canopy, foraging mainly for fruit, though you will sometimes see them feeding on the ground, especially during the rains when winged termites emerge for their "nuptial flight" and settle on open ground. They are also reputed to take nesting birds, small reptiles and roosting fruit bats, though their diet is overwhelmingly frugivorous. At feeding sites they might gather in groups of 10-20 but as a rule you will see them in pairs or small family units, basking in the sun, foraging high in the trees or flap-gliding overhead in their rapid, direct manner.

Another large and interesting bird found in the groundwater forest is the Crested Guineafowl. Flocks of these are not easily seen from a vehicle as they feed among the forest undergrowth and when disturbed tend to fly high into trees rather than run like their common, open-bush counterpart the Helmeted Guineafowl. The crests from which they take their name, to western Europeans of a certain age, might recall the kind of hats worn by elderly aunts in church.

The Forest Fringes and Mahali Pa Nyati

The forest eventually opens out and you find yourself at the first fork in the track. Most people turn left here to drive through the forest fringes, via Mahali pa Nyati (Place of the Buffalo) or its adjacent circuit to the Hippo Pool. Mahali pa Nyati is a large glade surrounded by woodland and shrubs, and well-named, though the buffalos which frequent the area are often out of sight, feeding by the inaccessible edge of the Simba River or resting in a smaller glade elsewhere.

The African Buffalo (*Syncerus caffer*) is another animal you can hardly miss in Manyara, even if you miss them here. Apart from its great size (male buffalos weigh up to 800 kg) they often associate in "breeding herds" which in Manyara can number in hundreds. Such herds consist mostly of females and young, the former recognisable (apart from their lack of obvious male appendages) by their lesser bulk and slimmer horns. There will be a number of bulls with the herds, though many older buffalo bulls go around in small "bachelor" groups, feeding on the sedges or lying around in mud wallows.

The buffalo is the main prey species for lions in Manyara, where wildebeeste are relatively few and where even zebras are difficult to hunt out of the open ter-

Left: Buffalo - main prey species for Manyara's lions

races by the lake. It is a formidable adversary, for its huge bulk is backed up by massive, sharply tipped horns and a determination, when wounded or threatened, to fight to the death. Someone once tried to organize a bullfight in Spain using an African buffalo as the bull, but no matadors could be tempted to take it on, which, when you consider the size and temper of the average Andalucian fighting bull, says a lot. The Manyara lions don't always have much choice, and they don't always win. You needn't worry about being hooked into eternity yourself; when unmolested, buffalos are usually as docile as Galloway cattle, though independent travellers shouldn't push their luck (the experienced driver/guides don't need to be told this).

One animal you will certainly see in this vicinity is the Impala *(Aepyceros melampus),* common throughout much of the park. Many tourists, after seeing and photographing impalas for the first time, move on, rarely giving the animals a second thought, which is a pity, as the impala is virtually a living fossil. Throughout an evolutionary period when some of its nearest relatives underwent almost twenty significant changes, the impala remained true to itself; even nature, it seems, cannot improve on perfection. And the elegant impala is surely as near-perfect as antelopes get. It is elegance in motion also, capable of leaping 3 m high and over 11 m in length, the equivalent of leaping over an elephant while clearing one-and-a-half cricket strips. This partly explains its evolutionary success, for there is an instinctive orientation in the leaps, towards other members of the group, one animal sometimes jumping over another in a predator-confusing explosion of movement.

Herds vary from a few to hundreds strong, mostly ewes (easily identified by their lack of horns)

under the watchful eye of a dominant ram, with young of both sexes, though you will also see herds composed entirely of males. Males often fight to acquire or maintain "harems", but fights are mostly ritualistic. The incumbent "harem masters" lose condition after a while, not through sexual exertions, for copulation is brief, but because of the constant need to chase or challenge rivals, or shepherd the ewes into compliance, and the distraction from feeding which this entails. Impala society, however, is far from simplistic and dominant males will sometimes allow bachelor groups to feed within their territory, providing they remain deferential.

The impala, being a ruminant or cud-chewing animal, has an interesting stomach as well as an interesting past. The ruminant stomach has four chambers, the largest of which, the rumen, first receives the hastily chewed food. But the fascinating thing about rumination is that it involves countless microscopic creatures, some of which break down cellulose. More remarkably, the bacteria

Top: Fascinating ruminant, the impala

include "carnivores" as well as "herbivores", and live only for about 24 hours, their dead bodies providing an astonishing one-fifth of the ruminant's protein requirements.

These open woodlands and forest fringes, interspersed with spacious grassy clearings and close to water, are ideal for impalas, and for a tree which is also common here, *Tabernaemontana usambarensis*. The Latin name is important, as its English name, the "Wild Mango", applies to several different trees. Which is why Carl Linnaeus, the 18th century "Father of Taxonomy", devised his system of according plants and animals classical names. This particular wild mango actually looks like its cultivated namesake, having similar leaves and attractive, fragrant-smelling white blossoms. Its fruits are somewhat different, however, growing in pairs joined at the base. They are dark green mottled with paler green and spherical to oblong in form, 4 to 6 cm long, giving rise, among old Africa hands, to the colloquialism "buffalo balls", which hardly flatters the tree. Or the buffalos. It doesn't bother the primates and hornbills which relish the many-seeded orange pulp. The tree, incidentally, is related to the desert rose and the exotic frangipani, both often found as garden plants in the tropics.

The woodland/grassland mosaic, perfect for buffalos and impalas, is also frequently used by zebras, though you will often see them in more open areas, partly because they are easier to see there but also because they probably feel more secure. The zebras belong to a race of Burchells *(Equus burchelli)*, though Manyara, biologically, is a transitional zone and debates continue about subspecies of certain forms. To non-biologists it might seem that "once you've seen one zebra you've seen them all" but this isn't so. Their stripe patterns, especially around the shoulder, are each distinctively different, as a little observation will confirm. Certainly zebras recognize members of their family group and perhaps a lot of others. Such family units, composed of two to six mares and a stallion, with whatever foals they have produced, are self-contained, despite the great congregations you might see in the Serengeti and elsewhere. The females in the zebra harem conform to a strict chronological hierarchy; when walking in characteristic single file they will be led by the "first lady", the mare which the stallion originally acquired, the other mares following in order of their "date of membership", with the stallion bringing up the rear.

Various theories have been put forward as to the purpose of the

zebra's bold striping. The latest seem to suggest that it confuses predators when a group of zebras explodes in panic during the predator's final rush, or that the contrasting stripes act as some kind of temperature control. Any photographer will tell you that the zebra was put on Earth to be endlessly photographed, the stripes evolving in anticipation of the auto-focus camera.

The Hippo Pool

The hippo pool is part of the Simba River, and its contours change as the river or the adjacent lake rises or falls. Sometimes it vanishes completely. Normally, however, it is quite accessible, though the treacherous nature of the alkaline mud which borders the river and lake doesn't permit too close an approach. Nevertheless, the car park, in this open area just beyond the southern limits of the groundwater forest, is near enough for you to get good views of the hippos and a wealth of animal and bird life, and safe enough for you to get out, stretch your legs and enjoy the scenery and spectacle at one of Manyara's most interesting and popular focal points.

Top: Strictly vegetarian hippo

The hippos are inevitably one of the main attractions. Familiar to the Ancient Egyptians and a crowd-pleaser since Roman times (hippos featured in the barbaric staged fights in the arenas) they are now popular for all the right reasons, though their huge, balloon-like figures and indolent lifestyle, and their frequent appearance as cuddly toys or cartoons, is deceptive. The Hippo *(Hippopotamus amphibius)* can move quickly and aggressively and must be treated with respect, ashore or afloat, though you are quite safe here if you don't wander far from your vehicle.

Strict vegetarians, hippos tend to leave the water at night to graze, though you will quite often see them out of the water by day in Manyara. At night they might wander quite far, consuming large amounts of grass and occasionally fallen fruits, though their daily intake is less than 1.5% of their body weight, compared with 2.5% for most other ungulates. Presumably the hippo's laid-back lifestyle and the fact that its weight is often supported by water reduces the need to eat more.

Certainly the hippo is in little danger of succumbing to anorexia or the protestant work ethic. Or to any predators other than humans, for though babies are sometimes killed a full-grown hippo is more than a match for lions and crocodiles, and in any case would hardly make an easy meal; its skin is 5-6 cm thick in places. Crocodiles, incidentally, are absent from Manyara.

Visitors often ask how long

hippos can remain submerged. In natural circumstances they rarely submerge for more than 3–5 minutes, increasing to 10 or more in more extreme situations. What is more certain is that hippos, with few if any exceptions, mate and give birth in the water. Which, when you are as heavy as a pick-up truck and built like a balloon, seems to make sense.

But the hippos are only a part of a much greater spectacle here by the pools. For in these wide-angled vistas, out on the grasslands and flats you will almost always see impalas, zebras, wildebeeste, giraffes, warthogs and perhaps buffalos and one or two elephants. More impressive still, on, around, over, above and beyond the pool, on grasslands and flats and along

the shallows of the lake as far as you can see, are countless numbers of birds, swimming, walking, standing, wheeling, landing, taking off, feeding, mewing, crying, squawking, raucously calling, muttering, chattering and squabbling in a living film-strip of sound and motion and muted colours.

In the foreground you might see Blacksmith, Crowned and Spurwing Plovers, with perhaps an African Pied Wagtail. On and in and around the pool will be geese and ducks and teal, storks, herons, egrets, ibis, spoonbills and avocets, cormorants, pelicans, pratincoles, thicknees, greenshanks, stilts and

Left: Hippos rarely submerge completely for more than a few minutes
Top: Flamingos en masse - an aesthetic delight

stints. And away in the distance, among all the other birds that feed or fish or forage in the shallows, huge swathes of flamingos, the pink froth on a very special cocktail.

Of all the birds to be seen here, perhaps the two favourites among non-specialists are the flamingos and the pelicans, almost certainly because each of them has been imprinted upon our imaginations since childhood, either through books such as "Alice in Wonderland", where a flamingo is used as a croquet mallet, or pic-tures featuring one or other of the two birds. Of course flamingos en masse are also an aesthetic delight, but close up they, like the pelicans, look ridiculous enough to appeal to our sense of the absurd, in the same way that warthogs do.

Be that as it may, both birds seem cheerfully familiar, even if we are seeing them in the wild for the first time. There are two species of each to be seen in Manyara, the Greater and the Lesser Flamingo and the White and Pink-backed Pelican. The Lesser *(Phoeniconaias minor)* is the

most numerous of the world's five flamingo species and the more striking of the two flamingos found in Africa, more richly flushed with pink and touched with carmine than its considerably larger cousin, and with a carmine bill. It isn't surprising that the very word "flamingo" comes from the Latin for "flame", *flamma,* a particularly appropriate derivation in the context of the Rift's origins. Nor is it surprising that the Ancient Egyptians regarded the flamingo as a living symbol of the sun god Ra, though the Greater Flamingo *(Phoeniconaias ruber)* is less "fiery" than the Lesser, being whiter with a pale pink bill. Nevertheless, its wing coverts and axillaries (the feathers covering the bases of the main wing feathers and those which grow between underwing and body) are a bright coral red.

Flamingos are as unusual as they look. They have longer necks and legs, in proportion to their bodies, than any other bird, and are believed to belong to one of the most ancient of bird families (which might explain why their brains are smaller than their eyeballs). But whatever they lack in IQ is made up for by their flamboyant plumage, the colour of which comes from carotenoid pigments (the most widely distributed of these being carotene, the pigment which colours carrots). In flamingos the pigments are derived from blue-green algae, consumed directly by the Lesser Flamingo and indirectly by the Greater, which feeds on brine shrimps which have absorbed algae. If there seems to be some frenzy in the flamingos' feeding behaviour it could be because success in courtship depends to some extent upon the individual's depth of colour; to be "in the pink", it seems, is essential to a lively sex life.

Left: Flamingos are as unusual as they look

Perhaps the most unlikely thing about these unlikely birds is their bill, which looks as ungainly and absurd as the birds themselves but which is a highly effective product of evolution. For flamingos are "pump and filter" feeders, their tongues acting as pumps and their upper and lower mandibles having rows of flexible plates, covered in fine hairs, which serve as filters. The tongue (incidentally considered a delicacy by the Ancient Romans) pushes whatever the bill picks up through the flexible plates, or lamellae, straining out the water or ooze, and the flamingo eats what remains. Even the strange kink in the bill has its purpose, ensuring that the bird doesn't take in too much water, and the upper mandible of the Lesser Flamingo, which unlike its counterpart feeds on floating matter, has air-filled cavities to give it buoyancy (its bill, like that of the Greater, being held upside down when feeding).

As if all this wasn't enough, the main breeding ground of East African flamingos is Lake Natron, 100 km north of Manyara, and one of the most inhospitable environments of Earth. Yet the fantastic flamingos take its many horrors in their considerable stride. They flourish in temperatures that can reach 65° C at the lake's surface and withstand levels of chlorides,

sulphates and fluoride that would be a cocktail of death to most other creatures.

The pelican isn't quite in the same league but it is most unusual nonetheless. Like the flamingo it looks as if it had been designed by someone with a rather wacky sense of humour, and like the flamingo it has a bill which has been fashioned by evolution in a very original way, though the pelican's lower mandible is not really used for storing fish, as is commonly supposed. At least, the peli-

can doesn't store fish there for long, swallowing them soon after capture by throwing up its head and tipping the fish down its gullet.

The adult White Pelican *(Pelecanus onocrotalus)*, sometimes known as the Eastern or Great White, is as big and white (with black wing tips) as the latter names suggests. Often well over 1.5 m long, it has a 3 m wing span. By comparison the Pink-backed *(Pelicanus rufescens)* is noticeably smaller, especially when you see the two species together, and pale grey rather than white, the vinous-pink rump which gives it its English name normally only visible in flight. Immature birds of both species might be confused, however, as those of the White are a pallid buffish-brown, those of the Pink-backed a pale grayish-buff, though the difference in size should help distinguish one from the other.

There is a difference in the feeding behaviour of the two

Top: White Pelicans (and black hippos)

species also. White pelicans characteristically fish in groups, cruising in inverted "V" formation, herding fish into the shallows and submerging their heads and necks in unison to catch them, as if choreographed. Pink-backed pelicans are solitary fishers, plunging at fish with heronlike stabs. It is quite fascinating to watch pelicans in action, especially the whites, not only on the water but in the air, as the whites, ungainly on land, look surprisingly graceful when flighting in to land, curving down like squadrons of beautifully controlled miniature flying boats. The Hippo Pool is an ideal place, incidentally, to get photographs of birds in flight, though remember that you might have to over-expose a little to make up for a bright background of sky or cloud. The opposite, incidentally, is true when photographing, for example, a dark buffalo or elephant against a relatively bright background.

Such birds as flamingos and pelicans are always popular but many keen birders get even more excited by a "little brown job" which might be encountered here, perhaps in quite large, scattered parties. When conditions are right along the lake shore, specifically when there is a lot of muddy grass, red-throated pipits, which breed in Eurasian tundra, might be added to your bird list.

Red-throated pipits or not, you can profitably and pleasantly spend hours in this lovely spot, with the pool and the lake before you and the Rift wall behind, and between them the grasslands and flats, half-encircled by woodland and forest. Most people see it in the morning, before setting off for Ngorongoro, but if you have time you should also come here in the late afternoon, before the sun slants down behind the escarpment and when the soft light of evening suffuses the lake, and the flamingos in the distance, with the

warmer colours of the spectrum. And talking of the setting sun, this is as good a place as any in which to enjoy the traditional East African sundowner, or a soft drink, or (this could go on and on!) a cup of tea or coffee.

Mkindu Drive

Assuming you visit the Hippo Pool in the morning and have time to spare, especially if you have brought a picnic lunch, there is much more of Manyara to see. If you continue around the loop beyond the Hippo Pool you will soon come to a "T-junction" where you can turn left, into Mkindu Drive. It might sound like an avenue in suburban Dar es Salaam but it is quite wild and atmospheric (especially if you meet a large bull elephant or a male lion coming the other way). It takes its name from the wild date palms (*Mikindu* in Swahili, singular *Mkindu*) which grow in some profusion here.

The Wild Date Palm *(Phoenix reclinata)* is closely related to the

---

Top: Elephant feeding by Mkindu Drive

commercially grown wild date, from which the generic name evolves. *"Phoenix"* alludes to an ancient myth, recounted here by the Latin poet Ovid:

"…one [creature] alone, a bird, renews and re-begets itself – the Phoenix of Assyria, which feeds not upon seeds or verdure but the oils of balsam and the tears of frankincense. This bird, when five long centuries of life have passed, with claws and beak unsullied, builds a nest high on a lofty sway-ing palm; and lines the nest with cassia and spikenard and golden myrrh and shreds of cinnamon, and settled there at ease and, so embowered in spicy perfumes, ends his life's long span."

What a way to go! Keen birders shouldn't get too excited; they are unlikely to add "Phoenix" to their list. But the wild date does have something in common with the palm which has been cultivated since Biblical times; its fruits are similar in appearance and edible, though smaller, less fleshy and insipid to the human palate. There is nothing insipid about the tree itself, though it is, quite literally, often "laid back", hence its specif-ic name. The "reclining" nature of the palm gives it particular grace in a family of trees well known for their elegance. It certainly adds to the charm of this particular drive, which takes you across a ford in the small Mkindu River and then across the similarly small and often dry Mchanga (Sand) River before curving around to rejoin the main track.

Elephants are particularly fond of the fruits of the wild date, and will often bring them down by shaking the palms vigorously; one reason why you are as likely to encounter elephants on this drive as anywhere else in the park, though the woodland here is quite dense so unless the elephants hap-pen to be on or alongside the track you won't see them. Or even hear them, for elephants, though they can be noisy, can also be as silent as a prayer.

They are, however, great com-municators, with a number of vocalizations, some below the range of the human ear. These infrasonic sounds bounce off "sonic ceilings" in the atmosphere, where two contrasting tempera-ture layers meet, enabling them to be heard by other elephants at great distances; some observations suggest 40 km, though more research on this fascinating phe-nomenon, only discovered in 1987, is needed. This might explain why elephants, from time to time, are seen to become agitat-ed for no apparent reason.

Left: Elephants - even big bulls like this - can be silent as a prayer

In the history section mention was made of Iain Douglas-Hamilton and his well-known study of Manyara's elephants in the 1960s. Iain, still heavily involved in elephant conservation, founded "Save The Elephants" in 1993 and among many other distinctions received one of conservation's highest honours, the Order of the Golden Ark. Sadly, many of the elephants he and Oria knew and loved were killed during the poaching outrages of the 1980s, though enough survived to ensure that these superbly "civilized" animals now roam Manyara's woodlands and forest in considerable and increasing numbers once again, to give pleasure to endless streams of visitors as they once gave to the Douglas-Hamiltons. Elephants also roam, as Iain found out, the less likely inclines of the steep Rift wall; looking for elephants high above your head is something of a novelty, but Manyara is full of surprises…

Iain's study was in many ways pioneering, especially in his methods of approaching elephants and identifying them. At a time when big game hunting was still regarded as a "manly" and dangerous business (which it often was) Iain's habit of driving into the midst of a family group and switching off his Land Rover engine while he took notes or photographs raised many eyebrows. And the blood pressure of some of his more nervous passengers, who would take comfort from the sight of Iain's gun, only to be told, on enquiring, that it was only carried (unloaded) as a matter of form.

But Iain, after a steep learning curve marked by some rather exciting moments, knew his elephants, which he identified by individual features, such as the outline of their ears, and by their tusks. He quickly discovered that elephants, as a rule, only show both tusks and extend both ears when they are charging (or pretending to charge) a trait not always conducive to calm concentration when attempting to photograph them. As elephants are remarkably easy-going, and astonishingly tolerant of human beings considering what we have done to them over the centuries, most confrontations were far less dangerous than they sometimes seemed. But there are always exceptions. Three cows which he called "The Tyrone Sisters" charged his Land Rover in the Endabash area, one pressing home the attack. Iain was lucky to escape with his life.

Such incidents are rare, even among people who work among elephants for years, and almost unheard of among tourists and other travellers, but independent drivers should treat elephants with

the respect they deserve and inspire. There is no real danger in being reasonably close to elephants in Manyara as long as you stay within your vehicle and don't block their progress or provoke them; even then they will usually just give you a warning trumpet and an angry shake of the head before making off. But don't take it for granted.

Characteristically elephants are calm and peaceful, and to spend a little time in their company, especially with your vehicle's engine switched off, its windows or hatch open and its passengers reasonably silent, is one of the joys of safari. You will find, to your delight, that you, like Iain and other researchers, will soon pick out physical peculiarities which would enable you to recognize certain individuals if you saw them again. And if the elephants are in a family group (the average size in Manyara is about nine or ten) you will also delight in the overwhelmingly quiet and dignified way in which elephants conduct themselves, especially towards each other.

It is common knowledge now that elephant society is matriarchal. The family groups just

Top: No real danger in being close to elephants if you use common sense

referred to will typically consist of the matriarch herself, two or three other adult females and their various calves, of different ages. Mostly you will see them browsing or grazing, for life is one long meal for a huge herbivore with an inefficient digestive system, but whatever they are doing, most first-time observers are immediately touched by the obviously close family bonds and by the predominant serenity of their lifestyles.

Tiny babies, if there are any, are highly popular among the family as well as the human onlookers, and as mischievous as most infants. Sometimes the tiny bulls will show off by "charging" your vehicle, trumpeting to awaken the dead but looking more like giant mice than monsters. But they are no lightweights; even new-born babies can weigh over 150 kg (330 lbs), considerably more than most heavyweight boxers. And they are almost a metre high. If infants seem small enough to pass beneath their mother's belly you can assume, roughly, that they are less than a year old. Tusks erupt at about 16 months of age but only emerge when the calf is about two-and-a-half. At around four-and-a-half to five it will often find itself with a new baby brother or sister, when its mother, with another mouth to feed and the older infant's 10-12 cm tusks poking her in the breasts (which incidentally are between her forelegs) will reserve her milk for the newcomer.

As well as shaking down wild dates the elephants sometimes turn their attention to another interesting tree which grows along and around this drive, the Yellow-bark Acacia *(Acacia xanthophloea)*. A medium to tall tree, it is much more attractive than its one-time common name ("Fever Tree") implied. This unfortunate misnomer was the result of guilt by association, as the acacia is a lover of low-lying swampy areas where mosquitoes breed. Even its characteristically yellow bark has inspired adjectives such as "evil", "pallid", "leprous", "sickly' and "sinister", none of which deter the elephants, which will peel off the bark in strips and eat it. The Yellow-bark is unusually rich in sugar, which might be part of the attraction. Many trees bear witness to this depredation, their trunks misshapen towards the base by gnarled old scars. Perhaps the sugar-rich acacia, which also exudes a gum popular with yet another of Manyara's monkeys, the Vervet *(Cercopithecus aethiops),* should be called the "Chewing Gum Tree"?

"Vervet" derives from the French word for "green" and refers to the monkey's coat, which is actu-

ally grey with a slight greenish tinge. The colour which surprises most human observers, however, is the bright turquoise blue of the adult male's scrotum, the Vervet's answer to the often quoted adage "If you've got it, flaunt it". These little black-faced monkeys are often found in acacia woodlands, and though frequently found on the ground rarely stray far from the safety of the trees. With good reason, for among Manyara's range of animals and birds are leopards, pythons, baboons and several large eagles, just a few of the creatures which the monkeys have to look out for. One of their greatest threats outside the parks comes from Man, not only through habitat destruction but because large numbers of vervets are shipped off each year to serve as the unwitting subjects of experiments in the world's medical laboratories.

Msasa River Area

On completing this lovely, leafy drive with its screens of palms, yellow-bark acacias and figs, you rejoin the main track and (assuming you head south) cross the Msasa River, *msasa* being the local name for a shrubby tree which grows here, *Cordia monoica,* former-

---

Top: Vervet monkeys are often found in acacia woodland

ly *C ovalis,* the *ovalis* referring to the oval leaves, which also give the small tree one of its common names, "The Sandpaper Cordia", as the upper surface of the dark green leaves are very harsh to the touch. The Maasai use the leaves to help preserve milk, and the fleshy, ovoid berries of the Cordia, orange-red when ripe, are edible.

Talking of things edible, there is a lovely picnic site above the Msasa (you will see the second of its two turn-offs, to the right, before reaching the bridge across the river, after which the campsite is named, having come on to the main track a little way beyond the first turn-off). There are tsetse flies on the picnic site but once you are out of your vehicle they don't bother you much, and the place is otherwise pleasant, with picnic tables and benches set out under a lovely old fig tree. There are basic toilet facilities here also. From one edge of the site you can look down into the Msasa Valley, where you might see elephants, buffalos, baboons or other animals, and also do some birding. Sometimes elephants, buffalos or lions visit or pass through the picnic site itself, but there is no danger as long as you are sensible.

Almost immediately after crossing the Msasa there is a loop road to the left which brings you to the lake shore, where you might see many of the birds discussed earlier in relation to the Hippo Pool. Among them might be one of the world's most unusual kingfishers, the Pied *(Ceryle rudis),* the largest bird (25–29 cm long) capable of hovering consistently in still air. This ability allows it to scout for fish over lakes, rivers or even the sea without the need for a perch. Incidentally many kingfishers take other prey as well as fish, and many of the forest or dry country kingfishers, such as the Woodland *(Halcyon senegalensis)* and Rufous-bellied or Grey-headed *(Halcyon leucocephal)* (both found in Manyara) feed almost exclusively on insects or small reptiles.

The Maasai Giraffe *(Giraffa camelopardalis tippelskirchi,* the only species found in Tanzania) is a browser, not a grazer, yet in Manyara you will often see them in open areas such as this, or even out on the treeless margins of the lake. Sometimes they are just passing through, sometimes, as by the Hippo Pool, they come to drink the fresh water, but like other herbivores, which don't always get enough salt in their vegetarian diets, they sometimes like to lick the salt-rich soils by the lakeshore.

Their main diet consists of leaves, especially those of certain

Left: Striking body pattern of the Maasai Giraffe

acacia, and here they are never far away from the extensive *Acacia tortilis* woodland, just to the south. As all acacias are armed with thorns one might think that meal times for the giraffe are fraught with painful possibilities, but if you watch a giraffe stripping acacia leaves from the branches with its extremely long (46 cm) tongue, you will see that they manage perfectly well, except in terms of actually getting enough to eat, for acacia leaves are tiny. Fortunately, despite their bulk, giraffes can maintain their condition on only 7 kg of foliage per day, though 30 kg is about the norm. They are ruminants, and where they feel secure you will sometimes see them sitting down to chew the cud.

As acacia leaves are often a long way from the ground, evolution, rather than trying to teach the giraffe to climb, made it into the tallest animal on Earth. Its neck is about 2 m long, and so are its legs (the front legs are only a little longer than the back, though an optical illusion, due to the giraffe's wedge-shaped body, makes them appear much longer). Even a new-born giraffe is 2 m tall. One would think that such a tall, large mammal would stand out like a lighthouse in the bush but evolution has taken care of that also, and giraffes, as you will find, often blend amazingly easily into their favourite acacia woodlands.

Acacia Woodlands

You are about to enter such woodlands, assuming you head south (left) when you arrive at the junction of the loop road and the main track. This is the beginning of a long and lovely belt of *Acacia tortilis,* over the branches of which the Manyara lions sometimes drape themselves. The archetypal "umbrella thorns" of the East African savannah, mature specimens are easily identified by their widely spreading, flat-topped crowns, their dark, deeply fissured bark and, when present, their tightly spiralled seed pods, popular with various herbivores. The acacia's most distinctive diagnostic feature, however, are its thorns. It has two kinds, one short and hooked, one long and straight. Noah is said to have built his ark out of the timber of this acacia, a handy thing to remember if you are in Manyara during the rains…

Maybe this is why the lions spend much of their time there; they want to be first in the queue when the next deluge begins, though the Manyara Noah would have to employ some delicate diplomacy if he resorts to the traditional "two by two" model; the 28 or so lions who miss the boat are hardly going to take the snub lying down…Though lying down is what lions do best, apart, perhaps,

Left: Lion at rest on the branches of an *Acacia tortilis*
Top: Buffalos relaxing at the edges of Lake Manyara

from mating; lionesses, like other female cats, need repeated sex to stimulate ovulation. One male in the Serengeti mated 145 times within 55 hours with one lioness, and 12 times with another. Mating takes only about twenty seconds but even so, weary dominant males sometimes give way to an eagerly waiting subordinate, with no obvious jealousy. And possibly much relief.

Lions might have an apparently "laid back" lifestyle but in Manyara they are, as we have seen, obliged to prey heavily on buffalos, which is rather more demanding than bowling over a wildebeest. There is at least one obvious advantage; buffalos have much more meat on them than smaller prey. Why go to the trouble of hunting two zebras or a dozen impalas when you can kill a single buffalo and then sit back and eat like a prince for days on end?

It doesn't take an Einstein to work out the drawbacks. Buffalos don't enjoy being eaten. Eight hundred kilogrammes of rancorous bone and muscle, with a huge and wicked pair of horns at one end, isn't going to surrender with an almost apologetic groan, like a wildebeest. Killing a buffalo requires different tactics and more lions. And, one would think, a huge amount of what in humans would be called "courage". Yet lions regularly kill full-grown buffalos in Manyara, and live to fight another day, though some of the struggles that take place, often in the secrecy of the woodland and forest, must be dramatic, and some of the encounters fatal for the lion, as well as the buffalo.

There are smaller, more delicate creatures in these acacia woodlands, as there are in the groundwater forest and elsewhere, for butterflies, representatives of an insect world which hums, buzzes, flutters and crawls in super abundance throughout tropical Africa, proliferate here as elsewhere. The butterflies, like their myriad insectile relatives, are most populous during and just after the rains, when their ubiquitous presence adds a welcome touch of fragility and colour, provided otherwise only by birds or flowers, to these strongholds of the dark and mighty.

Paradoxically it is the dark and mighty, in the form of elephants and buffalos, which help to sustain the "weak" (not that butterflies are inherently weak; considering their weight and composition they are amazingly strong and resilient). But not all butterflies feed on nectar from flowers; some feed on carnivore dung, others on the dung of herbivores such as the elephant, and moisture on the track, including elephant or buffa-

lo urine, often attracts clouds of butterflies, among them the large and beautiful swallow-tails.

Elephant dung is also popular with dung beetles, which come in a variety of shapes and sizes. A number of such beetles are capable of relocating a 7 kg heap of elephant droppings in less than an hour by rolling it into balls and burying them. More than 22,000 such beetles were once collected from a single pile of elephant dung within 12 hours, which says something about biologists as well as beetles. The more one learns about these creatures (the beetles, not the biologists), the more one understands why the ancient Egyptians considered one of them, the Scarab *(Kheper aegyptiorum)* sacred.

The Scarab comes in metallic green or violet, and is one of the "rolling dung beetles", the males of which you will sometimes see paddling a ball of dung along the track, looking for a "honeymoon suite" and followed by his would-be "bride". After burying the ball the two beetles mate in the hole and then, to make their day complete, enjoy a "wedding breakfast"

Top: Elephant droppings - more interesting than they might seem (if you are a dung beetle or butterfly)

of dung. They then make a second ball, kneaded into perfect roundness by the female. She makes a hollow in the ground and lays an egg, covering it with the ball of dung, now fashioned into a pear shape. Then goes off to repeat the process. The larva hatching from the egg eats the dung and pupates within its hard crust, emerging eventually as an adult beetle.

A wild gardenia grows throughout the acacia woodlands which, although not sacred as the Scarab was, is dedicated to Jove, head of the Roman gods. The spiky shrub, *Gardenia jovis-tonantis,* was so-named because rural Africans in Angola were in the habit of putting gardenia branches on the roofs of their huts, to prevent them being struck by lightning (Jove's traditional weapon was the thunderbolt). How the branches were supposed to deflect the lightning is another matter, but if they were in flower at the time the white blossoms, yellowing with age, they would at least have lent a touch of glamour to the family home. The ridged fruits of the gardenia, some 5 cm long and ovoid in shape, are eaten by elephants.

Elephants also enjoy the spherical wild cucumbers which you might also see here, growing on vines which festoon many trees and shrubs, but most browsers refuse to eat the smaller, yellow-coloured fruits of another plant found in the woodland and elsewhere, the Sodom Apple *(Solanum incanum)*. These fruits look a little like small, unripened tomatoes but in fact the plant is related to the potato. The ancient city of Sodom, by the Dead Sea, was said to have been destroyed by God, together with neighbouring Gomorrah, in retribution for the sins of its citizens. A marvellous plant with exquisite fruit was said to have sprung up where Sodom had stood. When the fruit was picked, it vanished in smoke, leaving ashes in the hand, and the so-called Sodom apple became a metaphor for something coveted, but once possessed bringing only disappointment. Or worse, for the *Solanaceae* family to which the present-day Sodom apple belongs has many poisonous members, including Deadly Nightshade.

Chem Chem, Ndala and Bagayo River Area

This area, which makes up the central sector of the park, is basically a continuation of the *Acacia tortilis* woodland, but being narrow it also brings you closer to the escarpment and the lake. Some 4 km south of the Msasa River you cross the Chem Chem and a further 2 km or so brings you to the Ndala, by which, further upstream,

the research centre where the Douglas-Hamiltons lived and worked is based. The centre is still in use but private, so please don't call unless you have been invited. You might see elephants or possibly lions by the Chem Chem or the Ndala, as elsewhere in the park. One animal you won't see, which was relatively common in Manyara a few decades ago, is the Black Rhino *(Diceros bicornis)* now locally extinct thanks to the ignorance, greed or desperation of those involved in its extermination.

But if you are extremely lucky you might come across another member of the so-called "Big Five" (which should be "The Big Six", including the cheetah, now that the camera has largely replaced the gun) and one that is much better at the survival game, despite being endangered because of its coat (and people who still find animal pelts attractive). The Leopard *(Panthera pardus)* might be shy and elusive (who can blame it?) but it has the widest distribution of all wild cats, surviving where other animals would have been wiped out long before, its habitat rang-

Top: Leopard gives itself a "cat-lick"

ing from near-desert to rain forest. Its catholic diet helps, for it can live off animals up to the size of impalas and sometimes beyond, right down to birds, dung beetles, frogs, crabs, pangolins, porcupines and even fish.

The leopard's well-known habit of hauling prey high into trees is probably a response to high concentrations of lions or hyenas, as in the Serengeti, though here in Manyara, with its huge biomass of big herbivores as well as lions and hyenas, there are other reasons for eating well above the ground. For the leopard this isn't a big problem; the versatile and charismatic cat is capable of hauling three times its own weight several metres up among the branches. Imagine picking up the equivalent of three suitcases, each weighing the regulation economy class maximum of 20 kg, at the same time, and you will get some idea of the strength involved. And this is without considering the near-vertical climb.

The narrow watercourses which break up the topological profile of Manyara, especially in its northernmost half, all screened by riverine woodland or forest, are ideal for leopards, but the cats would be almost as much at home among the boulders and scrub of the escarpment face, which closes in on you soon after you cross the Bagayo, 2 km or so south of the Ndala. From this point, about half-way down the length of the park, you get good views of the escarpment and its very different vegetation, among which, at this point, you will pick out the unmistakable Baobab (*Adansonia digitata*), standing out among the white-flowering, much-branching *Grewia tembensis* shrubs and the other hardy plants that survive on the steep rocky slopes. Down at ground level you are about to enter another very different kind of country.

Endabash Area

Where the park narrows you will pass the small hot water springs (Maji Moto Ndogo). The springs are fed by fresh groundwater which is heated as it circulates far below the surface, through fractures caused by the Rift Valley faulting. The temperature of the water at the springs themselves is about 40° C, a little above normal human body temperature.

These springs mark the beginning of the Endabash area, the relative broad, open country centred upon the Endabash River and covered by several loop roads as well as the main track. The area is characterized by rough-looking grassland and shrubs, among the most common being the Woolly Caper Bush (*Capparis tomentosa*). This small, leafy tree or prickly-stemmed climber is related to the shrub that grows wild around the Mediterranean and provides us with deliciously piquant capers. Its specific name (and the "Woolly" of its common one) refer to the densely velvety nature of the plant's parts when young. The fruits are sometimes produced in profusion, and when ripe are pink to bright orange, their flesh semi-transparent and grayish-blue. The leaves are said to be eaten by herbivores and (outside the park) by domestic stock but at least one authority describes the plant as highly poisonous.

In South Africa it is protected, and famous for its magical and medicinal properties, allegedly curing a host of complaints from the common cold to impotence. Among the more unlikely "cures" is one for pneumonia, which involves mixing parts of the tree with dried hyena and antelope blood, a remedy, one would think, not easily procured. A more acceptable "cure", especially during the long rains, is one believed to prevent floods. The trick is to coat a stick with paste made from the powdered roots and other bits of the caper, and point it at whatever storm clouds are looming. Much quicker, if less exciting, than building a Noah's Ark out of *Acacia tortilis…*

The predominant grasses here are of the drop-seed genus, *Sporobolus,* which belongs to a family all by itself, embracing at least 150 species. Common among these grasses by the Endabash is *Sporobolus pyramidalis,* or "Rat's Tail Grass" as it is called in some parts of the world. This robust grass grows to over one metre where circumstances allow and when young its seed head, which can grow to 40 cm long and 3 cm wide, resembles a rather large rat's tail. When flowering the seed head changes into an elongated pyramid (hence the specific name).

Trees in the area tend to be scattered and include the Sausage Tree *(Kigelia Africana),* with its surprisingly heavy, fibrous and sausage-like fruits hanging down from the dense green canopy, the Paperbark Acacia *(Acacia sieberana)* and the Desert Date *(Balanites aegyptiaca).* Among the various flowers and flowering herbs by the Endabash itself, especially during or just following the rains, are great clumps of convolvulus *(Ipomoea hildebrandtii),* related to the European Morning Glory and bindweeds. There are 89 species of *Ipomoea* in East Africa, some quite variable; the trumpet-shaped flowers of those here are generally white with purple centres and "veins", and collectively quite spectacular. Should you pull slightly off the track to stop or turn around you will also discover that at least one kind of wild sage grows here, the pungent, aromatic smell of its crushed leaves quickly pervading the air.

The Endabash is often a sand river, and out on the broad open sand or grassy terraces, or along one of the loop roads, which enable you to get closer to the Rift wall, the lake and certain reaches of the river itself, you might see a variety of game. One animal, especially by the river or its dry bed, might be the Common Waterbuck *(Kobus ellipsiprymnus)* distinguished from the similar Defassa Waterbuck (also found in Manyara, where the two overlap and perhaps hybridize) by the distinctive white ring encircling its rump, as opposed to the white rump patches of the Defassa. The Defassa *(Kobus defassa)* is far less often encountered in the park, but most experts now lump the two waterbucks together as one species. They are handsome, stately animals with shaggy, grey-brown coats, vaguely resembling the European red deer in form and size. But the waterbuck is a true antelope, as will be seen from the horns of the male, which are swept back, prominently ringed

and (unless broken off during a fight) permanent, whereas the antlers of deer are regularly shed.

Male waterbucks are very territorial and will occasionally fight to the death, and when wounded even attack a man. But they are generally placid, spending most of their time feeding peacefully, often on coarse, waterside grasses that other herbivores reject. For all their aggression when provoked, males will sometimes allow competitors to cross their territory in order to drink, providing the intruder shows due deference. Behaviour which confirms the importance of water to this well-named animal, which is rarely found very far from it. While waterbucks are nothing like as aquatic as antelope such as sitatunga or lechwe, they will wade into rivers or lakes if pursued by predators, their coat "waterproofed" by a greasy, pungent-smelling secretion. The flesh of older animals is said to take on this odour, making it less palatable to carnivores, though as carnivores often feed on rotting corpses they can't be too

Top: Defassa Waterbuck, which shares Manyara with its common counterpart

fussy. Lion and wild dog certainly kill and eat waterbuck from time to time.

Another animal found here as in other areas of Manyara is the Warthog *(Phacochoerus aethiopicus)*, inevitably, with its disproportionately large head and a face that only a mother could love, regarded with great affection by most visitors. It is certainly difficult not to smile the first time you see one, especially when it turns its back, after regarding you with short-sighted suspicion, and trots off, tufted tail sticking up like a rather tatty flag. Which is more or less what it is, a rallying point, in the long grass, for the tiny piglets which inspire further smiles and motherly sighs as they race after Mum.

Largely diurnal, warthogs spend most nights and the hotter

protocol to overtake or change position. Unlike Formula One drivers there is no champagne for the inevitable winner and in fact the warthog lifestyle, to humans at least, is rather less exciting than charging around the Nurburgring at 350 km per hour. Most of their day is spent grazing on short grasses, often kneeling to do so, or sometimes rooting for bulbs and tubers. If they are lucky they might also come across some fallen fruit, and like all pigs are not averse to gobbling up small mammals or carrion. Even elephant dung, rich in half-digested vegetable matter and protein, is grist to the warthog's digestive mill.

Hot Springs and Beyond

Beyond the bulge formed by the Endabash area the country closes in, reducing progress to a miniature switchback with twists and turns as the track traverses the boulder-strewn base of the Rift wall, with the lake not too far away to your left. Also to your left, below the track, you will see the main Hot Springs (Maji Moto). Don't expect anything as spectacular as the "Old Faithful" geyser in Yellowstone, but the springs are interesting and worth a little stop (you are allowed to get out here, if

parts of the day in their burrows. Piglets enter the burrows head first, while adults usually enter backwards, confronting would-be predators with an array of tusks, the lower pair of which have a vicious slashing edge. When racing for safety in typical single file each piglet usually has its own place in the running order, like Formula One drivers on the starting grid, except that it is against warthog

Left: Rather macabre advert for the Hot Springs

accompanied by an official guide and providing you don't stray too far). The small pools which make up the springs are similar to those of Maji Moto Ndogo referred to earlier, though more extensive and hotter (about 60° C). Apparently you could boil eggs in these pools within 30 minutes, but why anyone would do so when you can get perfectly good ones just down the track at the Tree Lodge is unclear. What might be more profitable is to examine the interesting algae that the springs support.

And if staring at algae doesn't have you writhing around in ecstasy, there is another distraction among the nearby rocks and boulders, that "ballerina of the bush", the Klipspringer *(Oreotragus oreotragus)*. Known as *"mbuzi mawe"* ("goat of the rocks" in Swahili), and "this darling little antelope" by the Victorian hunter Gordon Cumming, the Klipspringer lives up to all its nicknames. A little over half a metre high at the shoulder, and generally olive-yellow in colour, flecked with grey (the hairs, incidentally, are hollow), it is the only antelope adapted to a mountainous habitat. In the East African race females as well as males have short, spiky horns. Its agility among the rocks is astonishing, and you might see one or two of them perched on a huge, steep-sided boulder, balancing on the

tips of their hooves; hence the "ballerina". How they actually get up on to this particular rock is something to consider as you eventually drive on.

You will soon pass through another strip of *Acacia tortilis* woodland, with a few *A. sieberiana* mixed in, the grassy verges of the track often brightened by wild hibiscus *(Hibiscus vitifolius),* with translucent yellow petals and maroon centres. Apart from their beauty hibiscus are unique in that that when plucked (against regulations, of course, in the park) they remain fresh, without water, throughout the day. At night they quietly close and fade - don't we all? The *tortilis* acacias here are uniformly tall, perhaps because they regenerated at the same time on what was once farmland, a fact which accounts for the presence here of some jacarandas, exquisite when in blossom elsewhere but less welcome exotics in Manyara. The woodland is home to about 120 olive baboons.

Some 13 km south of the Endabash you will cross a smaller river, the Yambi, and a further 1.5 km brings you to the delightfully secluded Tree Lodge, at the extreme southern end of the park. The lodge, less than 1 km from the lake, is set among beautiful woodland dominated by Cape mahogany, with some sausage

trees, wild mangoes, blue-stem cordia, sycamore fig and desert date. Clusters of climbing, deep purple *Thunbergia* sometimes enhance the glade in which the lodge is situated.

Mammals to be found in or close to this woodland include elephants, buffalos, hippos, impalas, bushbucks, waterbucks, warthogs, olive baboons, and blue and vervet monkeys, with lions and leopards often visiting the locality (there is a resident lion pride in the nearby Endabash/Hot Springs area). A much smaller cat-like creature, the lithe Large-spotted Genet *(Genetta tigrina)* also occurs here, though it is related to the mongooses, not the cats. And two galagos, or bushbabies, might be seen (or heard!) in the woodland around the lodge. One is the Greater or Thick-tailed *(Galago crassicaudatus),* the other the Small-eared *(Otolemur garnetti),* once classed with *crassicaudatus* but is now regarded as a separate species.

Bushbabies get their name from their best-known cry (one of many). One expert writes of "crescendo calls" lasting for as long as 20 seconds, building up to

Top: Klipspringer - "this darling little antelope"

a "paroxysm of sound", a description which anyone who has been awakened at night by small babies will immediately recognize. And like many small babies, galagos urinate a lot, though the bushbabies pee over their hands as well as for relief, to mark their territories among the trees in which they live. Bushbabies have other unusual abilities. They can rotate their heads through 180°, like owls, can hear a cricket walking 5 m away and their huge eyes can distinguish shadowy objects up to 30 m (98 ft) away, even by starlight. They are omnivorous, feeding largely on insects but also on gum exuded by acacias (or when they can get it, jam or honey from a lodge kitchen; at least one bushbaby, in the Selous, was found the next morning with its head stuck in a jam jar, from which it was extricated (cautiously, as bushbabies have a pretty serious bite). And finally, it seems that among bushbabies, size doesn't matter after all; it's the structure which counts. At least for researchers, who sometimes rely on the structure of a bushbaby's penis, as well as its highly individual call, to identify it.

This southern woodland is also home to some beautiful and interesting birds. Among them are the Purple-crested Turaco, Silvery-cheeked Hornbill, Green Pigeon, Green Wood Hoopoe, Peter's

Twinspot, Eastern Nicator, Grey-olive Greenbul, the African Wood Owl and the Narina Trogon (named by the intriguing 18th century French naturalist François Levaillant after his Hottentot mistress). Along the forest edges keen birders might see the Spotted Morning Thrush (or better still hear it, for it has a most mellifluous song), the Slate-coloured Boubou or the Ashy Starling, common in nearby Tarangire but on the edge of its range in Manyara and only found in the southernmost sector. Ashy starlings are

only found in Tanzania, and although obvious where they occur, comparatively little is known about them.

The Marang Forest

At the time of writing (June 2005) the Marang Forest above the escarpment is not part of the park, though it might be soon. As well as its variety of interesting trees and other plants, it is an important refuge for certain large mammals, such as elephants, many buffalos and bushbucks, bushpigs, leopards, olive baboons, blue monkeys and vervet monkeys, and of course various smaller mammals, insects etc. Bird life is reported to be "brilliant" (in more ways than one, it seems, as the colourful Schalow's Turaco, Bar-tailed Trogon, White-tailed Blue Flycatcher and the Oriole Finch are among the Forest 'specials'). As well as the less colourful but no less exciting Grey-headed Nigrita (Negro Finch), Montane White-eye and the Black-fronted Bush-shrike.

Top: Rift wall at sunset

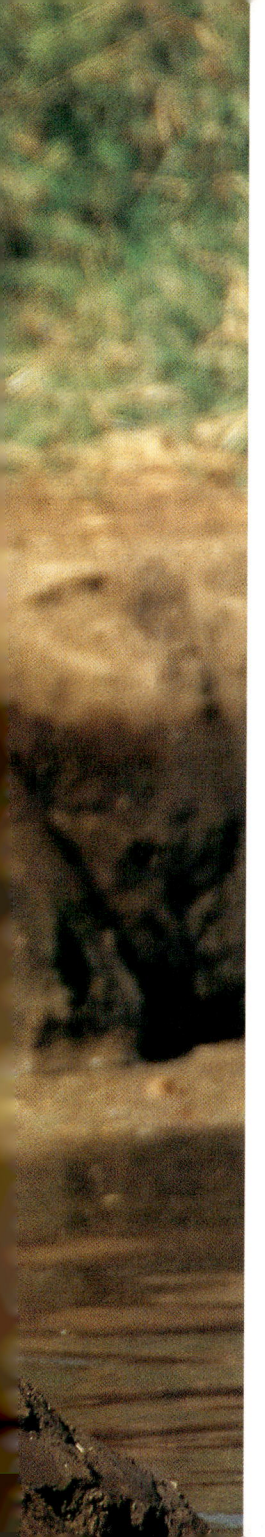

POSTSCRIPT - MANYARA'S OTHER BIRDS

This sector, kindly donated by a keen birder, is necessarily limited, as are the Tree Lodge/Marang Forest lists given previously. But together they should provide a helpful introduction for other birders, experienced or merely enthusiastic.

The woodland/bush/grassland mosaic which makes up much of Manyara is rich in birdlife, unlike the groundwater forest, and much more accessible to visitors than the Rift wall. What follows are some of the more conspicuous and unusual species, but the selection is, of course, arbitrary and limited.

Eurasian Bee-eaters are common on passage in Tanzania but scarce during the northern winter; Manyara is one place where they are regularly seen. During the same season Blue-cheeked Bee-eaters are sometimes common - they favour the lake edges more than the bush.

Even non-birders are likely to notice the Red and Yellow Barbet because it looks as if a child has painted a black and white bird with red and yellow spots and splodges. Further south it is

Left: Scratching an itch

replaced by the almost as gaudy Crested (or Levaillant's) Barbet, but Manyara is one of very few places where both species occur. A similar, but smaller and less colourful barbet, Darnaud's, also occurs; these may be a separate species from those in the Serengeti - the Usambiro Barbet. Pairs of all these barbets call in duet, the performance of Red and Yellows being especially appealing. Another member of the family, the White-headed Barbet, is more of a forest bird, with a limited distribution: the local race has a completely white tail and is unmistakable.

The Magpie Shrike, rare farther north, is perhaps the most striking of its family. The Long-tailed Fiscal Shrike is even showier; groups gather for what appear to be tail-twirling competitions. The Taita Fiscal, here at the southern edge of its range, is easy to tell from the Long-tailed Fiscal in theory but less so in practice, at least on first acquaintance; the Taita is smaller, has white in the tail and is much less gregarious.

The longclaws in Manyara are Pangani, not a rare species but much less widespread than the Yellow-throated. North American birders will think them remarkably like meadowlarks, which are not even closely related. This is a wonderful example of parallel evolution, and it is interesting to consider why these birds should be almost identical in colouration.

The long-tailed sunbirds are mostly birds of higher latitudes than the park, but the aptly named Beautiful Sunbird is fairly common in acacia woodland. It is one of the species in which males have a non-breeding plumage. Golden-winged sunbirds, incidentally, might be seen in the gardens of the old Lake Manyara Hotel, on the rim of the Rift wall, as well as elsewhere. Both sexes have golden wings and the male retains his long tail throughout the year.

The Steel-blue Whydah, the dullest but rarest of the whydahs in East Africa, is found in Manyara. Like cuckoos and honeyguides, whydahs lay their eggs in the nests of other birds. But, unlike cuckoos and honeyguides, baby whydahs do not eject or kill their foster-siblings, but are raised with them; that the young of he parasite resembles the young of the host to an astonishing degree, even to the call and the marking inside the gape, must be a factor in this attractive example of co-existence. Incidentally, the only known host of the Steel-blue Whydah is a waxbill, the Black-cheeked, not found in Tanzania, but it is almost certain that the very similar Black-faced Waxbill raises the baby whydahs in Manyara.

The Yellow-billed Oxpecker is rarer that the Red-billed Oxpecker in most of East Africa; both are found in the park. Both find buffalos and giraffes rewarding (if reluctant) hosts, but it seems that only the Red-billed habitually settles on hippos. Oxpeckers are never seen on elephants, which apparently do not need them and are obviously well-equipped to repel them, but they will feed on just about every other large mammal. However, there is one exception; waterbucks resist thcir attentions vigorously, and will even run off to escape what are to most antelopes helpful visitors; it is believed waterbucks produce their own insect repellent.

Top: Brown Snake Eagle devouring snake, in the groundwater forest

ACCOMMODATION

Lake Manyara Tree Lodge

The only lodge within Manyara, situated in the park's relatively remote and less-visited southern corner. Owned by Conscorp Africa, which has an excellent reputation, the lodge's seclusion, among a grove of mature forest trees between the Rift wall and the lake, is one of its main assets. But it also offers comfortable and interesting accommodation in the form of 10 tree houses, built in African mahogany trees, superb food and top class guides. Great place for birders as well as big game enthusiasts. Game drives, bush walks, birding safaris, picnics by the lake available if required.

www.ccafrica.com

Lake Manyara Serena Safari Lodge

Part of the well-known and reputable Serena chain. Wonderfully friendly, well-run lodge in an excellent situation, overlooking the Great Rift Valley and the northern sector of the park, just 15 minutes or so drive from the park gates.

Left: View towards Lake Manyara

Accommodation in well-appointed, "African style" rondavels with balconies looking out over the valley and lake. The lodge gardens are mainly composed of natural bush, to conform to Serena's sincere policy of ecologically-inspired "development", and therefore good birding is available on the doorstep. Excellent food and service. Game drives (in park), bush walks (by the lodge), cultural visits, mountain-biking and canoe safaris (on the lake) available if required.
www.serenahotels.com

Lake Manyara Hotel

Lake Manyara Hotel is the longest-established of the hotels and lodges in the area, and like many of the hotels and lodges that were first to be built in or alongside any of the parks or other tourist attractions, it has an outstanding location, directly overlooking the northern sector of the park and the lake. Once belonging to and managed by the state, it has been through a period of rehabilitation but is now thriving under new ownership. All rooms provide memorable views over the Rift Valley – as do the superb terrace and swimming pool areas.
www.hotelandlodges-tanzania.com

Kirurumu Tented Lodge

As with all the top-of-the-escarpment lodges, Kirurumu has fine views over the Rift and towards the head of the lake. Accommodation in large, walk-in luxury tents. Well-run camp with a welcoming and unpretentious atmosphere, set, like the Serena, among natural bush. Good food, comfortable accommodation. Activities include mountain-biking, ethno-botanical bush walks by the camp, horse-riding, cultural visits, fly-camping in forests and 1–5 day walking safaris up the extinct volcano Lossiming or down in the Rift, or to various other interesting areas.
www.kirurumu.com

E Unoto Retreat

Relatively new luxury camp at the foot of the Rift wall, to the north of the park and about 25 minutes drive from the park gate. Entirely inspired by the Maasai and their culture, the camp has a number of spacious, comfortable bungalows, located by a papyrus swamp and small lake. Among the Retreat's various interesting features are its large beds (which at least one guest has described as "the best in Africa"). Other attractions include a small swimming pool, mountain biking, bird-

watching, nature walks (including treks up the escarpment area) and cultural visits, especially those involving the local Maasai.
www.maasaivillage.com

Migunga Forest Camp

Situated amid an extensive grove of *Acacia seyal* woodland two kilometers from the shore of Lake Manyara, 10/15 minutes drive outside the park gate via the nearby village of Mto wa Mbu. Rustic in concept, the camp offers a simpler, cheaper but comfortable alternative to some of the other lodges. The camp has a number of self-contained tents, with hot and cold water and flush toilets in the bathroom sectors. Electricity is provided by solar power. Thatched dining room and bar. Bushbucks and other antelopes sometimes seen in or by the camp, bushbabies may be seen every evening at dusk. Activities include birding, cultural tours and guided walks through the woodland and if required out on to the lakeshore. Trek from Empakaai Crater in Ngoro ngoro to Lake Natron in the Rift also available on request.
www.safaris-tz.com

Low Budget Alternatives

There are several guest houses and camps in the village of Mto wa Mbu, just outside the park. Among the better ones is Twiga Guesthouse and Campsite, just off the main road. Accommodation includes basic but clean rooms and a selection of pleasant camping areas. Restaurant serves simple, reasonable food and there is a bar. Another possibility is the Fig Tree Campsite, in a similar location.

Other low budget options open from time to time, and standards in established ones often change for better or for worse, so travellers are advised to seek the latest information as and when they can, and to shop around for themselves.

PARK MANAGEMENT AND CONSERVATION

I n a book such as this, intended for the caring, well-informed but non-specialist visitor with limited time, the topic of park management and conservation can only be discussed briefly. This is not to minimise the importance of the subject, only to acknowledge its complexities.

One of the greatest changes in park management and conservation policies over the years is that which gradually evolved from solutions imposed arbitrarily from outside ("Fortress Conservation"), with little if any consultation with local people, to the modern belief that the co-operation of such people is vital to successful management and conservation.

All Tanzanian parks now have some form of "outreach" programme, in which various dedicated organizations and individuals, from within the parks and from outside, work with local villages towards a better understanding of the authorities' and the villagers', problems and objectives, in an interactive and hopefully sensitive way. Manyara is no exception.

Left: Zebras, and their habitats, need all the help we can give them

Main Conservation Issues

Among the main concerns with regard to conservation of the Manyara ecosystem is the threat of deforestation within the catchment area, leading to probable siltation problems, and the threat to the integrity of the important wildlife corridor that links Manyara with Tarangire National Park.

Another concern has to do with pressures due to rapidly increasing human populations just outside the park. The one-time small village of Mto wa Mbu, right outside the park's northern boundary, has expanded considerably in recent years and, with the upgrading of the road between it and Makayuni, seems likely to grow at an even faster rate.

Meanwhile, up on the Mbulu Plateau, which adjoins the park boundaries along the upper edge of the Rift Wall, the average household of the Iraqw farming people who dominate the plateau numbers over seven individuals, contributing to a very high and escalating population density and a growing hunger for land. These pressures pose a particular threat to the Marang Forest Reserve that presently lies between the edge of the Rift Wall (where it coincides with the park boundary) and the Iraqw farmland.

A rather different problem,

though due to similar pressures, is the fact that many large mammal species are genetically isolated within the relatively small and narrow confines of the park, with the obvious likelihood of inbreeding that this implies.

But Manyara is as important for its birds as it is for such mammals, with the lake and its margins, as well as the Marang Forest, being particularly vulnerable. The Groundwater Forest within the park is also a vital breeding site for Pink-backed Pelicans and Yellow-billed Storks, together with lesser numbers of Marabou Storks and Grey Herons.

All these factors need to be

addressed by present and/or future management plans. The Marang Forest should be declared part of the park as soon as possible, and the inclusion of the whole of Lake Manyara into the park should also be seriously considered (this could be done without denying local fishermen the right to operate in certain areas of the lake on a sustainable basis).

The wildlife corridor between Manyara and Tarangire should be freed from all threats of cultivation or similarly inappropriate encroachments, and extended wherever necessary (so as, for example, to include the Acacia seyal woodlands to the north-east of the lake).

The extensive swamps to the south of the lake should also either be included within the park if possible or given more official protection.

Manyara's relatively small size (by African standards) makes it easier to manage in some respects, more difficult in others. Only determined action now will prevent an inevitable and probably irreversible decline of its ecosystem.

Top: Manyara is as important for birds as it is for mammals
Next: Lions and cubs at home amongst the branches

Bibliography

Among the Elephants (Iain and Oria Douglas-Hamilton) – Book Club Associates
Antelopes (C A Spinage) – Croom Helm
Birds of East Africa (J G Williams & N Arlott) – Collins
East Africa (Jan Knappert) - Sangam Books
Field Guide to the Larger Mammals of East Africa (Dorst & Dandelot) – Collins
Maasai Women (Ulrike von Mitzlaff) - Trickster Tanzania Publishing House
Mammals of Africa (Haltenorth & Diller) – Collins
National Parks of East Africa (John G Williams) – Collins
Ngorongoro's First Visitor (Baumann, Organ and Fosbrooke) – Conservator, NCU
Tanzania - African Eden (Javed Jafferji/Graham Mercer) – Gallery Publications
The Behaviour Guide to Africa's Mammals (Richard Estes) – Russel Friedman
The Kingdon Field Guide to African Mammals (Jonathan Kingdon) – A & C B
Tanganyika Notes & Records (various editions) – Tanganyika Society
Trees of Southern Africa (Keith Coates Palgrave) – Struik
Wild Flowers of East Africa (Michael Blundell) – Collins
Wild Lives (Doreen Wolfsen McColaugh) – African Wildlife Foundation

Useful Distances (approximate)
Manyara Main Gate to/from:

Dar es Salaam	768 km	(485 miles)
Arusha	125 km	(79 miles)
Makuyuni	44 km	(28 miles)
Mto wa Mbu (Centre)	5 km	(3 miles)
Karatu	22 km	(14 miles)
Gibbs Farm	27 km	(17 miles)
Manyara Serena Lodge	8.3 km	(5.2 miles)
Lake Manyara Lodge	8.3 km	(5.2 miles)
Kirurumu Camp	8.3 km	(5.2 miles)
Lake Manyara Tree Lodge	39 km	(24.6 miles)
Lodoare Gate (Ngorongoro main gate)	38.5 km	(24.3 miles)
Naabi Hill Gate (Serengeti NP)	152 km	(96 miles)
Seronera (Serengeti NP)	200 km	(126 miles)

KIA Lodge Kilimanjaro International Airport

Moivaro coffee plantation & lodge
Arusha

Moivaro Coffee Plantation
Lodges & Tented Camps
TANZANIA

Fumba Beach
Zanzibar

Lake Manyara

Serengeti

Lake Natron & Oldonyo Lengai

Outdoor activities & excursions

Your African escape

Maasai culture

Introducing your hosts

E Unoto Retreat

www.maasaivillage.com
eunoto@maasaivillage.com

"E Unoto" is one of the Maasai's most important ceremonies It is a joyous occasion during which warriors choose the wives and enter into junior elder-hood Singing, dancing and counseling accompany this month long celebration May your stay at E Unoto Retreat be a joyous occasion.

The lodge

Your honeymoon

Photo gallery

Location

Conferences & incentives

Rates & reservations

Contact us

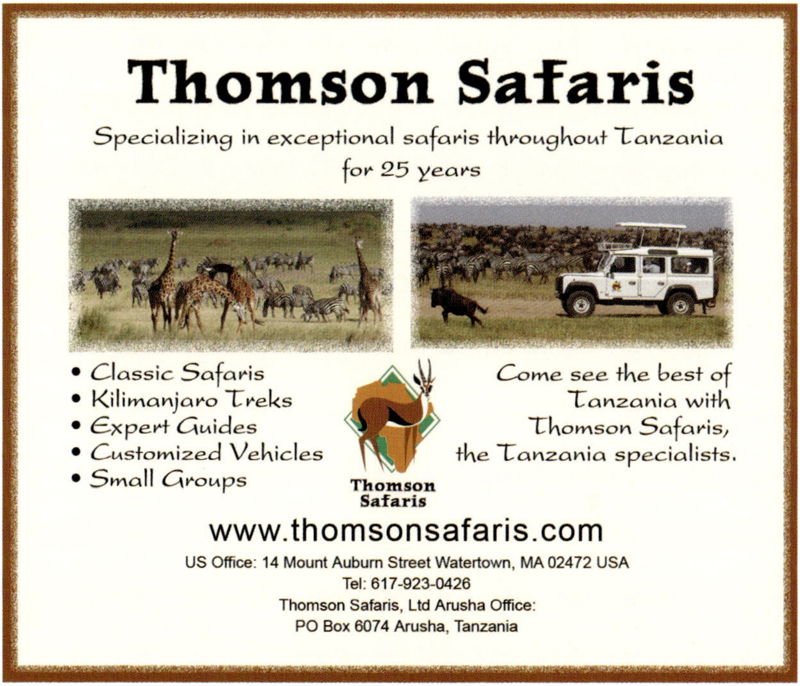
Thomson Safaris
Specializing in exceptional safaris throughout Tanzania for 25 years
• Classic Safaris
• Kilimanjaro Treks
• Expert Guides
• Customized Vehicles
• Small Groups
Thomson Safaris
Come see the best of Tanzania with Thomson Safaris, the Tanzania specialists.
www.thomsonsafaris.com
US Office: 14 Mount Auburn Street Watertown, MA 02472 USA
Tel: 617-923-0426
Thomson Safaris, Ltd Arusha Office:
PO Box 6074 Arusha, Tanzania

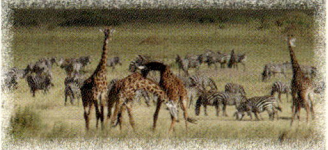

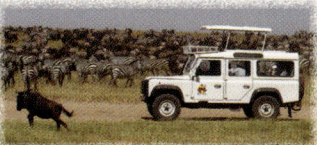

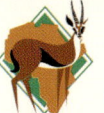

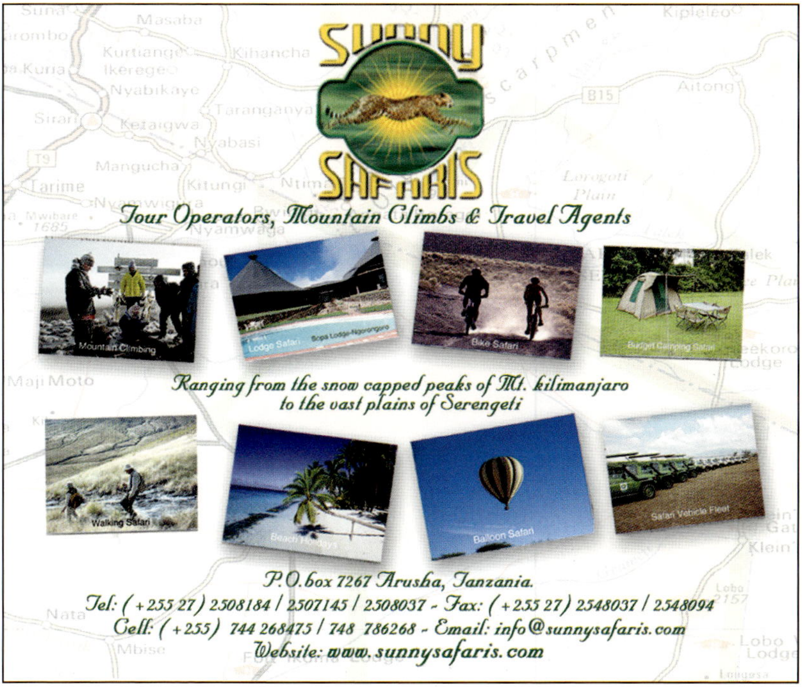
Sunny Safaris
Tour Operators, Mountain Climbs & Travel Agents
Mountain Climbing
Lodge Safari
Bike Safari
Ranging from the snow capped peaks of Mt. kilimanjaro to the vast plains of Serengeti
Walking Safari
Balloon Safari
Safari Vehicle Fleet
P.O. box 7267 Arusha, Tanzania.
Tel: (+255 27) 2508184 / 2507145 / 2508037 - Fax: (+255 27) 2548037 / 2548094
Cell: (+255) 744 268475 / 748 786268 - Email: info@sunnysafaris.com
Website: www.sunnysafaris.com

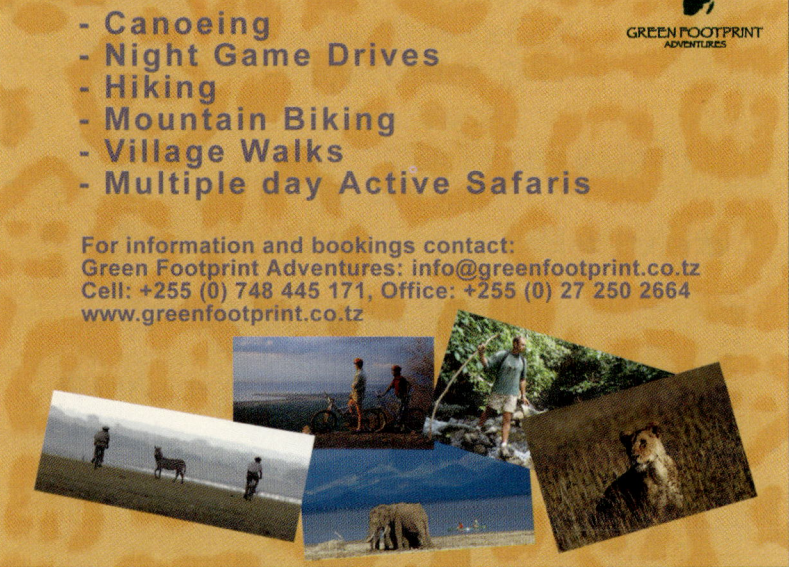

OTHER BOOKS PUBLISHED BY
GALLERY PUBLICATIONS

A Taste of Zanzibar - Zarina Jafferji & Javed Jafferji
A mouth-watering selection of Zanzibar's finest recipes to set your taste buds tingling with memories of your stay in Zanzibar.

Dhow Chasing in Zanzibar Waters - Captain G L Sullivan
An action-packed autobiographical account of the efforts of a British naval Captain to help suppress the illegal slave trade in the Indian Ocean.

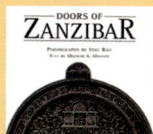

Doors of Zanzibar - Mwalim A Mwalim
Celebrates the intricate detail and beauty of Zanzibar's carved wooden doors, exploring Indian, Arabic and Swahili influences. Illustrated with stunning photographs.

Historical Zanzibar - Romance of the Ages
Professor Abdul Sheriff & Javed Jafferji
Illustrated account of Zanzibar's turbulent past, with archive photographs of the slave and ivory trade, life in the palace, the Shortest War in History and colonial rule.

Images of Lamu - Elie Losleben & Javed Jafferji
Images of Lamu is a photographic book of the culture, history and architecture of Kenya's northern archipelago. A UNESCO World Heritage Site, Lamu has captivated travellers for generations.

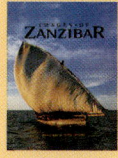

Images of Zanzibar - Bethan Rees Jones & Javed Jafferji
Glossy coffee-table book packed with stunning photographs from across Zanzibar and Pemba, including Stone Town, landscapes, beaches, culture and aerial shots.

Life of Frederick Courtney Selous - J G Millais
Autobiography of the famous hunter, explorer, naturalist, patriot and pioneer, providing a glimpse into the life of an extraordinary Englishman in the heyday of colonial Africa.

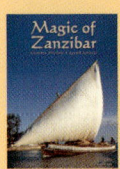

Magic of Zanzibar - Gemma Pitcher & Javed Jafferji

A handy pocket-sized book of photographs for visitors to take home. Zanzibar's architecture, natural history, culture and colourful people are all depicted in full colour.

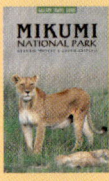

Memoirs of an Arabian Princess from Zanzibar - Emily Reute

Written by Princess Salme, who eloped with a German trader, this autobiography provides an absorbing account of life in the harem and the palaces during the sultanate rule.
Also available in French, Italian, Spanish and German

Mikumi National Park - Graham Mercer & Javed Jafferji

For too long Mikumi has been one of East Africa's most underrated parks. This book should change all that. It includes a fascinating history of the area as well as many insights into the park itself and superb photographs.

Ngorongoro Conservation Area - Graham Mercer & Javed Jafferji

What more can be written about this jewel in Tanzania's tourist-attraction crown? Quite a lot, as this book shows. Much of the information will be new to many people, and the entire Conservation Area is covered.

Ruaha National Park - Graham Mercer & Javed Jafferji

Ruaha is one of East Africa's finest parks and one of its wildest. Why do so many "old Africa hands" love it? This book and its wonderful photographs might provide the answer.

Saadani National Park - Dr Rolf Baldus, Vanessa Beddoe & Javed Jafferji

Saadani is one of Tanzania's newest national parks and the only one where the bush meets the sea. This travel guide covers the dramatic history, wildlife and fauna of this little-known and unique part of Tanzania.

Serengeti National Park - Graham Mercer & Javed Jafferji

The Serengeti, with its astonishing seasonal migration, is the world's most famous national park, yet this new guide book treats it in a refreshingly individual and interesting way, with up-to-date information and stunning photographs.

Selous Game Reserve - Dr Rolf Baldus, Ludwig Siege & Javed Jafferji

The Selous is the largest protected area in Africa and home to the most spectacular wildlife. This travel guide contains everything the visitor needs to know and is the only reliable source of information on this little known destination.

Safari Elegance - Amanda Harley & Javed Jafferji

Capturing the spirit of romance and adventure in the heart of the African wilderness, Safari Elegance celebrates the best of Kenya's safari design against the dramatic backdrop of the country's diverse landscape.

Safari Kitchen - Amanda Harley & Javed Jafferji

A glossy coffee-table style cookbook featuring the very best of Kenya's safari cuisine. Fabulous still-life shots of prepared dishes are combined with images of unique dining experiences in the heart of the wilderness.

Safari Living - Gemma Pitcher & Javed Jafferji

Stylish coffee-table book exploring the neglected area of Tanzania's design heritage, celebrating the style of the country's luxury safari lodges and private homes.

Safari Living Recipes - Gemma Pitcher and Javed Jafferji

Accompanying 'designer' cookbook featuring handpicked recipes from Tanzania's top safari lodges and camps.

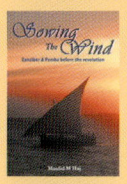

Sowing the Wind, Pemba before the Revolution - Maulid M Haji

Autobiographical novel exploring life and politics through the eyes of its central character, Maulid, in the turbulent years leading up to independence, and the subsequent revolution in 1964.

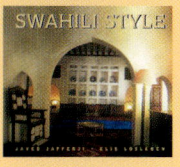

Swahili Style - Elie Losleben & Javed Jafferji

Swahili Style covers the design and architecture of the Swahili coast of Kenya and Tanzania, featuring exclusive properties and private homes that have been inspired by the stone towns and coral palaces of the Indian Ocean coastline.

Swahili Kitchen - Elie Losleben & Javed Jafferji
Swahili Kitchen features the best of Swahili cooking as served in the area's best lodges. From the beaches of Kenya and Tanzania, full menus using island spices and fresh Indian Ocean catch are a perfect way to remember East Africa.

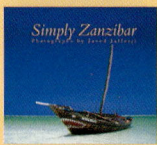

Simply Zanzibar - Gemma Pitcher & Javed Jafferji
A lush, full colour coffee-table book celebrating the unique visual appeal of the Spice Islands Zanzibar and Pemba.

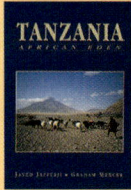

Tanzania African Eden - Graham Mercer & Javed Jafferji
Beautifully illustrated and well-written tribute to Tanzania's many attractions, in coffee-table format – a wonderful gift for anyone living in Tanzania, visiting it or for armchair travellers who want to experience this astonishing part of East Africa.

The Autobiography of Sir Henry Morton Stanley
Sir Henry Morton Stanley's biography takes readers on a journey from his destitute beginnings spent at a poorhouse in Wales, to shores lined with slaves in Zanzibar, and onwards through the wilds of the 'dark continent' and beyond.

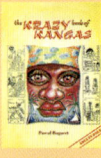

The Krazy Kanga Book - Pascal Bogaert
A distinctly off-beat book looking at some of the more bizarre aspects of East Africa's favourite garment - the kanga. Illustrated with lively and entertaining sketches showing the endless uses for kanga and how to wear them.

Tippu Tip, His Career in Zanzibar and Central Africa - Dr Heinrich Brode
New edition of Dr Brode's highly readable account of the life and times of Zanzibar's most notorious slave trader.

Tarangire National Park - Graham Mercer & Javed Jafferji
For years Tarangire was almost unknown except to a few "old Africa hands" who were happy to have the place to themselves. That has now changed and more tourists are discovering the park each year. This book and its fantastic photographs should help to explain why.

Zanzibar Tales - George Bateman
A lively and entertaining translation of Swahili folktales passed down from generation to generation.

Zanzibar, A Plan for the Historic Stone Town - Francesco Siravo & Stefano Bianca
Packed with historical information, plans, photographs and illustrations, this reference book takes a detailed look at Zanzibar's history and architecture, and the future preservation of Stone Town.

Zanzibar in Contemporary Times - Robert Nunez Lyne
Focuses on the nineteenth century, detailing the consolidation of Omani Arab power from the Gulf to Zanzibar, the arrival of the British, and the struggle against the slave trade.

Zanzibar - Island Metropolis of Eastern Africa
First published in 1919 and written in the style of the times, Zanzibar - Island Metropolis of Eastern Africa explores the fascinating history, culture and landscape of Zanzibar, and is a fascinating piece of history in its own right.

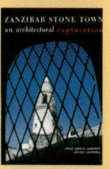

Zanzibar Stone Town, An Architectural Exploration - Professor Abdul Sheriff & Javed Jafferji
A pocket-sized guide examining the unique blend of architectural styles that make up Zanzibar's historic quarter, illustrated with sketches and colour photographs.

Zanzibar Style - Gemma Pitcher & Javed Jafferji
A sumptuous full colour coffee table book celebrating the natural style of the island's inhabitants, exploring themes inspiring Zanzibar's architecture and interior design.
Also available in Spanish, French, Italian and German

Zanzibar Style Recipes - Gemma Pitcher & Javed Jafferji
Accompanying 'designer' cookbook featuring a selection of dishes from Zanzibar's upmarket hotels and resorts.

Zanzibar - An Essential Guide - Amanda Harley & Javed Jafferji
All the essential information for visitors seeking to discover this tropical paradise along with fantastic photographs.

All books distributed by:
Zanzibar Gallery
Mercury House, P O Box 3181, Zanzibar
Email: gallery@swahilicoast.com

You'll never want to check out.

Spectacular scenery. Rich wildlife. Cool breezes. Nothing quite compares to Serena's Safari Lodges in East Africa, the ancestral homes of the Masai tribe. You'll be stunned at how our lodges are ingeniously designed to blend with the environment, while offering you the very best in five star luxury. Call us now for an experience you'll never want to leave.

SERENA HOTELS

KENYA · TANZANIA · ZANZIBAR · MOÇAMBIQUE

For reservations please contact your travel agent or Serena Sales centre on

Serena Central Reservations Nairobi Kenya: PO Box 48690, 00100 Nbo, Phone: +254 - 020 - 2711077/8, Fax: +254 - 020 -2718103, Email: cro@serena.co.ke, Website: www.serenahotels.com

Serena Central Reservations Arusha Tanzania: PO Box 2551 Arusha Phone: +255 - 272 - 506304/508175, Fax: +255 - 272 - 504155/504058, Email: reservations@serena.co.tz

Serena Hotels Johannesburg, Reservations Office Phone: +2711 327 2991, Fax: +2711 327 2998, Email: polana@icon.co.za

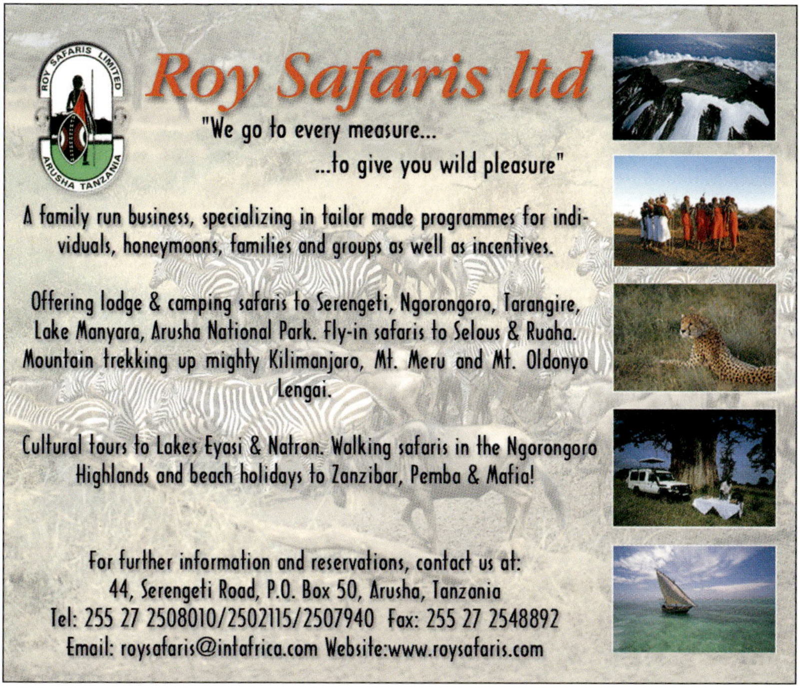
Roy Safaris ltd
ROY SAFARIS LIMITED
ARUSHA TANZANIA
"We go to every measure...
...to give you wild pleasure"
A family run business, specializing in tailor made programmes for individuals, honeymoons, families and groups as well as incentives.
Offering lodge & camping safaris to Serengeti, Ngorongoro, Tarangire, Lake Manyara, Arusha National Park. Fly-in safaris to Selous & Ruaha. Mountain trekking up mighty Kilimanjaro, Mt. Meru and Mt. Oldonyo Lengai.
Cultural tours to Lakes Eyasi & Natron. Walking safaris in the Ngorongoro Highlands and beach holidays to Zanzibar, Pemba & Mafia!
For further information and reservations, contact us at:
44, Serengeti Road, P.O. Box 50, Arusha, Tanzania
Tel: 255 27 2508010/2502115/2507940 Fax: 255 27 2548892
Email: roysafaris@intafrica.com Website:www.roysafaris.com

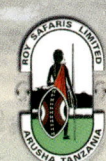

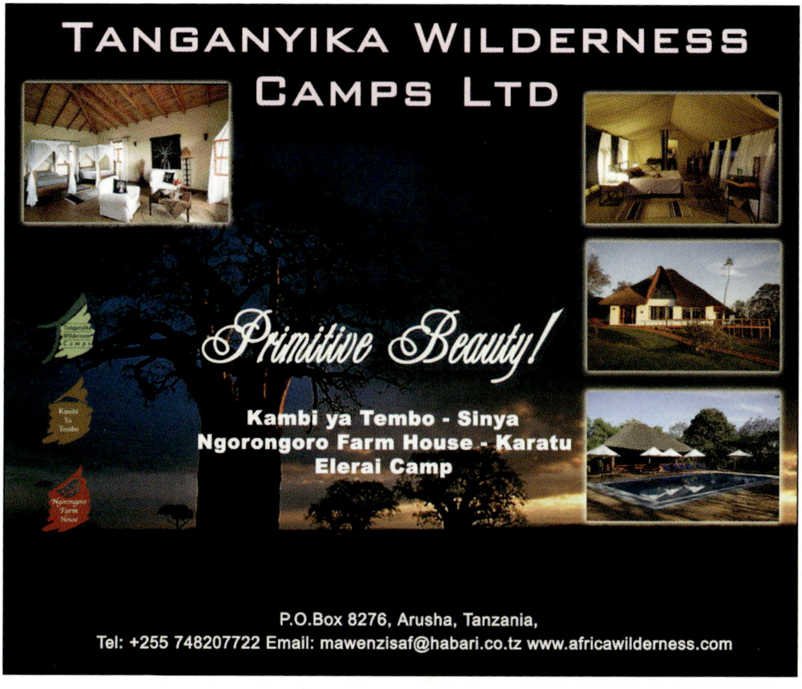
TANGANYIKA WILDERNESS CAMPS LTD
Primitive Beauty!
Kambi ya Tembo - Sinya
Ngorongoro Farm House - Karatu
Elerai Camp
P.O.Box 8276, Arusha, Tanzania,
Tel: +255 748207722 Email: mawenzisaf@habari.co.tz www.africawilderness.com

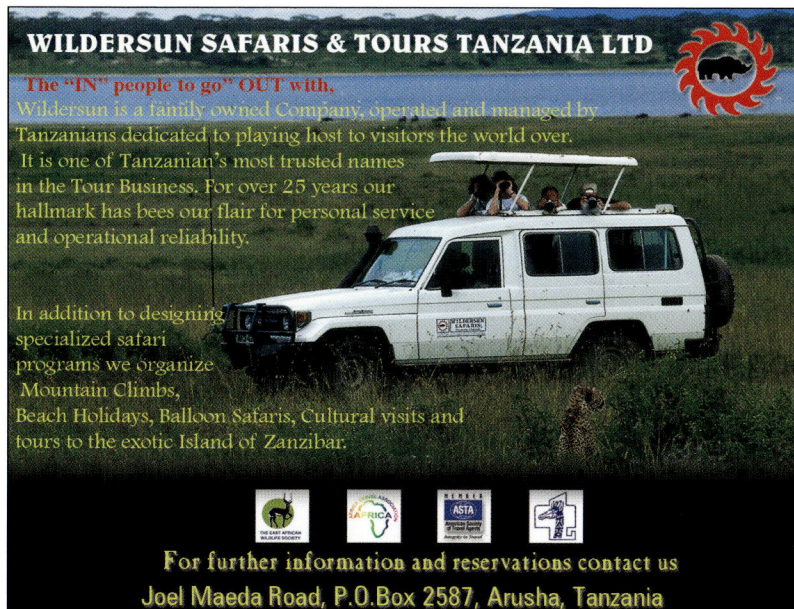

INDEX

About the Author

Graham Mercer experienced his first East African safari as a young sailor with the British Royal Navy in 1962, in Kenya, and has visited Lake Manyara many times. Throughout his 28 years in Tanzania he has been based at the International School of Tanganyika in Dar es Salaam. He has visited all the Tanzanian national parks.

The BBC Wildlife Magazine, after he won its prestigious essay-writing prize in 1988, referred to him as one of "Britain's best nature writers". Since then he has had ten books published, all on Tanzania, and held and participated in several photographic exhibitions.

Many of his articles and photographs have appeared in wildlife and travel magazines, local and international.

About the Photographer

Javed Jafferji studied photography, film and television in the UK, before returning to Tanzania, where he has now published over 30 books on the wildlife, landscape, culture and style that makes East Africa so unique.

Based in Zanzibar, Javed also publishes a magazine called the 'Swahili Coast', manages a photography and design company, and runs the Zanzibar Gallery, a shop selling antiques, books, gifts and clothing.